HISTORY of HEARTBREAK

by
Dan Whenesota

Minneapolis, Minnesota

Dedication
To Thomas and Charity.

Acknowledgments
The author wishes to thank the following: Mom and Dad for being Minnesota sports fans; Will for the push; Ricky Cobb from Super 70s Sports for the inspiration; Dan Barreiro and Justin Gaard for giving "The Calendar" a voice; Scott Korzenowski for the interview; the lunch crew: Paul, Matt, Houa, and Kyle; Joe for taking care of my family; Matt K. for the social media advice; Mary Ann Mancini for the North Stars games; and all the WHENESOTANs who can laugh about it—especially those who submitted calendar entries, even though we couldn't include them all in this book.

Edited by Ryan Jacobson. Proofread by Emily Beaumont, Cheri Jacobson, and Jennifer Mitchell. Fact-checked by Natalie Fowler. Cover design by Ryan Jacobson and Shane Nitzsche.

The following images are copyright 2020 The Associated Press: Minnesota Vikings: Brett Favre (front) by Paul Abell, Minnesota North Stars (front) by Elise Amendola, Minnesota Twins (front) by Ann Heisenfelt, Minnesota Vikings: Gary Anderson (front) by Morry Gash. For additional photography credits, see page 255.

The information presented in *History of Heartbreak* is accurate to the best of our knowledge. However, the information is not guaranteed. It is the sole responsibility of the reader to verify the information before relying upon it.

10 9 8 7 6 5 4 3 2

ISBN: 978-1-940647-41-8
eISBN: 978-1-940647-42-5

TABLE OF CONTENTS

FOREWORD

The first time I covered a football game in the Metrodome was January 3, 1983. I was working for the *Dallas Morning News*, and on that occasion, Tony Dorsett took a handoff out of the Cowboys' end zone and galloped 99 yards for a Cowboys touchdown. It was the longest run from scrimmage in NFL history—and the Vikings were facing an offense that had only 10 players on the field.

Little did I know that almost four years later, I would return to Minnesota as a sports columnist for the *Star Tribune*, with the chance to sit next to Sid in the Metrodome press box for the next quarter-century. And little did I know that this moment of sports infamy, which served as my introduction to the Minnesota sports scene, would so aptly capture a market's identity of fear and loathing.

I might not be one of us, but it did not take long for me to get to know and even to understand a fundamental, all-consuming Minnesota sports psychosis: If it can go wrong, it will. Often in record-setting, mind-blowing, never-before-seen ways that have stood the test of time, not just locally but nationally, maybe even cosmically.

I was in the Dome to chronicle World Series titles in 1987 and 1991, which surely indicated that the worst-outcome notion has not always applied. (And later, the Lynx became a WNBA dynasty.) Yet the swings and misses—in Super Bowls, in NFC title games, in NBA draft lotteries, in Herschel Walker trades, in Joe Smith secret deals, in Whizzinators, in sex boats, in academic frauds, in franchise departures, in so many ways—are so plentiful and rich and powerful that they, more than anything else, mold the character of your average Minnesota sports fan.

It is an essential part of being a Minnesota sports fan. Sometimes, I wonder if he or she would even know what to do if they lost that part of their identity.

And so, over the years, delving into that character and the sports events that forged it, peeling away the layers became a crucial part of my column style at the *Star Tribune* and then an essential trademark of my show, *Bumper-to-Bumper*, on KFAN Radio. I guess it's the ambulance-chaser in me, the Danny Downer.

Which brings me to Dan Whenesota. As we both recall it, one Sunday morning in October 2018, I asked listeners to submit their most painful sports nightmares. Dan blew me away not by submitting a handful but by sending me an entire calendar of nominees. Every month, every sport, in some cases every calendar day.

I started calling it the Calendar of Calamity and drew from it sometimes almost daily. Dan kept adding to it and building upon it, and now it takes its next logical turn. It becomes an absorbing, all-too-relatable, Shakespearean tragi-comedy with chapters such as "Court Jesters," "Disorder in Dinkytown," and the inevitable "Purple Haze."

Here's the beauty of it: No matter what Minnesota sports generation you are a part of, you will be able to relate to the pain. From Sir Francis demanding a trade to 12 Men in the Huddle, from the Lakers and North Stars leaving to the Timberwolves being sold to out-of-town ownership to Carl Pohlad threatening to move or contract, it's all covered. From Kirby Puckett's forced retirement to the Burnsie expletive tirade (after a victory, no less).

This is a historical homage to heartache.

It borders on the absurd, what has gone wrong, really, and the way some calamities inspired several others, mistakes piled on top of blunders. Dan doesn't just find the obvious ones— which he details —he finds the nooks and crannies. The hidden gems. Or should it be hidden atrocities?

If the rest of the country cared enough about us—and we know they don't; we remind ourselves of that reality every day, living in flyover country; we revel in our insecurity, which is why We Like It Here and even put it up on a sign in the Metrodome— this would be a 30 for 30 waiting to happen. Maybe even a 10-parter called *Why We Can't Dance*.

The point, I think, of his useful exercise isn't to torture the Minnesota sports fan. It is, rather, to prod the fan to laugh to keep from sobbing. It is to remind folks that though this might seem serious stuff, this isn't COVID-19 serious. That in the end, this is, after all, the toy department.

It is to demystify these momentous calamities, bring them to life in a way that, for better or worse, simply make them unforgettable and make the Minnesota sports fan say, "You want to know why I'm the way I am? Why I carry with me a pervasive sense of dread? Why I'm often sullen and withdrawn? Why I expect the rug to be pulled out from under me? This is the why."

Over the years, in print, on the air, and online, it has been hinted at, touched upon, and explored.

Here, it is captured, nailed, drilled down upon like never before, brought to life in ways that might indeed be painful but are also unforgettable.

I may not be one of us, but I know who you are.

So does Dan Whenesota.

— Dan Barreiro

INTRODUCTION

"Fan" is short for "fanatic," which implies a lot of emotion. We Minnesota sports fans have endured a wide range of that. Just check social media after one of our team's losses. It's like the five stages of grief. There's anger, sadness, and even denial. After every new collapse, we go through each stage again and again, one by one.

This book is about the "acceptance" stage. For me, though, acceptance often comes out as laughter. Dark humor maybe, but it's laughter nonetheless. At some point, you have to be able to take a step back and see the hilarity in the "here we go again" of it all. I felt no anger or negativity while writing this. It was therapeutic for me, and hopefully it is for you— and even our teams, as well. *History of Heartbreak* is about bravely facing our past and moving forward, all while laughing about it together. After all, laughter is the best medicine, and it's certainly healthier than sadness or anger.

This book is also about hope. It's not easy being a Minnesota sports fan. We're extremely loyal; we stick with our teams through the bad times and the good. We know that the chance of getting our hearts broken again is extremely likely, yet somewhere, deep down, we still believe that this could be the year. So we watch. After all, without hope, why bother paying attention?

In an effort to exorcise our demons, I created a documentary film called *WHEN-ESOTA?*, about the heartbreaks of being a

Minnesota sports fan. To promote the film, I started a blog on which I posted my ramblings about different Minnesota-sports-related topics. One of those blog posts was called "On This Day in Minnesota Sports Disappointment History." It was a calendar of eye-rolling, face-palming events that happened in our sports past. This book is an expanded look at several events on that calendar.

The idea is to look back at our collective misery in a light-hearted way. Some events are heartbreaking. Some are just silly. However, there's a fine line between what's considered humorous and what crosses the line. Some events in our sports history are unsavory. Abuse and harassment of any kind aren't funny. In fact, they're despicable. Those events are not a part of this book.

With that said, let's forge ahead together. Lie back on the WHEN-ESOTA? therapist's couch and relax. (I have a B.S. in psychology; you can trust me.) Kick up your feet, read on, and let the healing begin. . . .

— Dan Whenesota
Whenesota.com

ABOUT WOMEN'S SPORTS

I'm often asked about women's sports. In short, I'm a huge fan. I've coached girls' and women's sports for more than 20 years, so I understand how important inclusivity is. Having said that, our Minnesota women's teams are not included in *History of Heartbreak*. Why? Because this book is about disappointment and heartbreak. Our women's sports teams are successful.

They may not win every game or every championship, but they have a consistent history of winning. The Minnesota Lynx won four WNBA championships over a span of seven years. The Minnesota Whitecaps won the NWHL championship in 2019 and were set to make another run in 2020 before the pandemic shut down all sports. The Minnesota Vixen professional football team won two conference titles and made it to the 2018 Division II WFA championship. The Minnesota Golden Gophers volleyball team made a sixth trip to the Final Four in 2019, and the Gophers women's softball team made it to the Women's College World Series in 2019. The Gophers women's hockey team has won seven championships, including one in 2016. The Gophers women's basketball team advanced to the Final Four in 2004 (and didn't need anyone to do their homework).

How can we call all of that success "heartbreaking"? The only disappointing aspect of our women's sports is that they aren't celebrated more. So, needless to say, they don't deserve the *WHEN-ESOTA?* brand of ridicule.

— Dan Whenesota

ACRONYMS & ABBREVIATIONS

AL: American League (of Major League Baseball)

CB: Cornerback (football position on defense)

DE: Defensive end (football position on defense)

DT: Defensive tackle (football position on defense)

LB: Linebacker (football position on defense)

MLB: Major League Baseball

MVP: Most Valuable Player (award)

NBA: National Basketball Association

NCAA: National Collegiate Athletic Association

NFC: National Football Conference (of the NFL)

NFL: National Football League

NHL: National Hockey League

NL: National League (of Major League Baseball)

OT: Offensive tackle (football position on offense)

QB: Quarterback (football position on offense)

RB: Running back (football position on offense)

S: Safety (football position on defense)

U of M: University of Minnesota

CHAPTER 1
THE DIRTY DOZEN

At my website, www.Whenesota.com, the Minnesota Sports Disappointment Calendar contains more than 400 entries. (You might better recognize it as the "Calendar of Calamity"—affectionately dubbed by KFAN Radio's Dan Barreiro.) That's too many entries for one book. With help from a handful of friends and sports fans, I narrowed them down. Together, we selected the "big ones," those that were most heartbreaking, bizarre, and shocking. Then I created a survey on social media, and I asked fellow WHENESOTANs to rank them. All of that data was crunched and averaged. Following are the 12 most heartbreaking events in Minnesota sports history, as determined by our entirely unscientific rankings and survey results. Feel free to disagree. After all, half the fun of sports is debating topics just like this.

#12: FIRST OVERALL DRAFT PICK ELUDES WOLVES FOR 26 YEARS

 1989–2015

HEARTBREAK RATING:

> WHAT HAPPENED:

In the early 1980s, the NBA rewarded its worst team by giving them the first overall pick in the next draft. This created an incentive for bad teams to "tank," or lose games on purpose, in order to acquire the best college player. To combat this, the NBA implemented a draft lottery system in 1985. The worst team is still the most likely to get the top pick, but it is no longer guaranteed. A few weeks before each draft, the league holds its lottery to determine the draft order for all 14 non-playoff teams from the previous season. The lottery hasn't been kind to the Minnesota Timberwolves. Our team finished with the worst record in the league three times, but the number-one overall pick eluded us until 2015. Even in the 1989 NBA Expansion Draft, Minnesota selected second out of two teams (page 84). Plus, throughout the Timberwolves' first 30 drafts, the lottery never helped us move up. We either stayed where we were originally slotted to pick or fell down the draft board.

> WHY IT HURT SO MUCH:

The NBA draft lasts only two rounds, and usually there are only a few franchise-changing players. By not having a first overall pick for so long, the team missed out on some all-star players.

For example, the Timberwolves finished last in the 1991–1992 NBA season, with a 15–67 record. During the draft lottery that followed, the Timberwolves "won" the third overall pick. The Orlando Magic selected Shaquille O'Neal with the first pick. The Charlotte Hornets got Alonzo Mourning with the second pick. Minnesota drafted Christian Laettner. In 2011, the Wolves once again finished with the worst record, yet we received the second overall pick. Cleveland was awarded the first, and they selected Kyrie Irving. The Wolves chose Derrick Williams.

> THE AFTERMATH:

The Timberwolves currently have the worst all-time record in the league, winning about 40% of our games. In the franchise's first 29 seasons, we made the playoffs nine times. We were victorious in the first round of the playoffs once, in 2004, when the team advanced to the conference finals (page 91).

> DAN'S NOTES:

The whole point of expansion is to create franchises that can be successful, in order to increase the popularity of the league. It's shameful that it took 26 years for an expansion franchise to get a number-one overall pick. It isn't difficult to find theories about rigged lotteries online, including articles from reputable sources like CBS Sports. After all the bad luck we've had, it's sometimes hard to dismiss those rumors out of hand.

#11: THE PHILADELPHIA FAIL: VIKINGS MISS SUPER BOWL LII

 January 21, 2018　　　　HEARTBREAK RATING:

> WHAT HAPPENED:

The Minnesota Vikings were coming off a dream season. In storybook fashion, reserve quarterback Case Keenum led the team to a 13–3 record and the number-two seed in the NFC playoffs. In our first playoff matchup, the Vikings were victorious against the New Orleans Saints in one of the greatest games in NFL history (now known as the "Minneapolis Miracle"). The Vikings were down by a point with 10 seconds left in the game. Keenum threw a deep sideline pass to receiver Stefon Diggs at the 35-yard line. Diggs caught it, stayed in bounds, and avoided a Saints defender. He ran into the end zone and scored the winning touchdown. That play vaulted Minnesota into the NFC Championship. The Vikings were favored by three points over the Philadelphia Eagles, largely because Minnesota was up against the Eagles' backup quarterback, Nick Foles. Our fans were so confident that they visited Philadelphia's Rocky Balboa statue and dressed him in Vikings apparel. In the game, we took the lead on the opening drive when Keenum threw a 25-yard touchdown pass. But we wouldn't score again. The Eagles put 38 unanswered points on the board. Foles threw for 352 yards and three touchdowns.

> WHY IT HURT SO MUCH:

Things like the Miracle weren't supposed to happen to the Vikings. We're the team on the other end of that. Because of that play, some fans started to believe again. They thought our fortunes had turned. This Philadelphia Fail was a very harsh reminder from the football gods. Eagles defensive end Derek Barnett caused a fumble late in the first half that thwarted a Minnesota rally. In a cruel twist of fate, the Eagles had selected him with a 2017 draft pick that we traded to them (for quarterback Sam Bradford). The Eagles went on to win Super Bowl LII against the New England Patriots, 41–33 . . . at U.S. Bank Stadium in Minneapolis. Yes, we were forced to watch the Eagles win the Super Bowl on our home field.

> THE AFTERMATH:

A few days after the Super Bowl, the Vikings hired Eagles' quarterback coach John DeFilippo as our offensive coordinator. He didn't last a season; he was fired after Week 14. Keenum and Diggs won an ESPN ESPY Award for the year's "Best Moment." The Vikings did not re-sign Keenum, opting instead to sign free agent Kirk Cousins to a three-year, $84 million deal.

> DAN'S NOTES:

After the Miracle, I was not a hopeful fan. I felt like we had narrowly escaped Death, and it would come looking for payment. When our fans dressed up Rocky Balboa, I knew this game was going to be ugly. Philadelphia fans have a bad reputation. To me, messing with Rocky was poking the bear.

In 2017, Case Keenum and the Vikings were 13–3 in the regular season.

#10: BASEBALL VOTES TO CONTRACT . . . THE TWINS?

 November 6, 2001   HEARTBREAK RATING:

WHAT HAPPENED:

The term "contraction" in sports means to eliminate a franchise. It wasn't a new term in 2001; MLB contracted four teams way back in 1899. The ugly term reared its head again in the 1990s. In 1995, the Minnesota Twins claimed that they couldn't be competitive in the current stadium—the Hubert H. Humphrey Metrodome—so they wanted a new one. A few proposals went before the Minnesota Legislature, but none were passed. In 1997, Twins owner Carl Pohlad was given permission from the league to sell the team (page 120). There were a few potential buyers, but the Twins remained in Minnesota. Then rumors of contraction began to swirl.

On December 18, 2000, the *Star Tribune* quoted Pohlad as saying that he wanted no part of contraction and that his objective was to keep baseball in Minnesota. On October 23, 2001, reports surfaced of contraction occurring, with the Montreal Expos and Florida Marlins getting cut. A few days later, the Twins were rumored to be one of the teams. On October 31, Pohlad angrily denied that he volunteered for contraction. On November 6, MLB owners voted 28–2 to eliminate two franchises. On that same day, the Metropolitan Sports Facilities Commission (MSFC) filed a lawsuit to force the Twins to honor their lease at the Metrodome.

> WHY IT HURT SO MUCH:

Minnesota had already endured two teams leaving: the Lakers (page 80) and the North Stars (page 36). The Timberwolves were also threatening to go (page 86). It felt like the Minnesota sports scene was getting turned on its head.

> THE AFTERMATH:

On November 16, 2001, a Minnesota judge granted the injunction filed by the MSFC to force the Twins to stay put for the 2002 season. The Twins and MLB appealed the decision. On January 22, the Minnesota Court of Appeals ruled in the MSFC's favor. The issue moved to the State Supreme Court. On February 4, the Court refused to hear the appeal. The next day, MLB commissioner Bud Selig called off contraction. That April, the *Star Tribune* reported that the Twins organization had been discussing contraction as early as April 2001. The team won 94 games in 2002—and the AL Central Division title. We beat Oakland in the AL Division Series, three games to two. During the post-series celebration, Pohlad admitted to volunteering the team for contraction. The Twins fell in the AL Championship Series to the Anaheim Angels. In February 2006, a Hennepin County District Judge gave Pohlad permission to sell or move the team. In May 2006, the "Ballpark Bill" was passed, paving the way for Target Field to be built.

#9: GOPHER MEN'S BASKETBALL PROGRAM CAUGHT CHEATING

 March 10, 1999   HEARTBREAK RATING: ♥♥♥♥♥

> WHAT HAPPENED:

The NCAA Men's Division I Basketball Tournament is one of the biggest events on the sports calendar. Getting invited into the tournament is like being in the playoffs. Advancing all the way to the Final Four is akin to playing in the World Series or the Super Bowl. In 1997, the Minnesota Golden Gophers made it to the Final Four.

In 1999, the team qualified for the tournament again. However, on March 10, the day before we were to play our first tournament game, the *Pioneer Press* reported that a former U of M employee named Jan Gangelhoff did coursework for basketball players. It was also alleged that she had done so since 1993 and that U of M officials—including head coach Clem Haskins and academic counselor Alonzo Newby—were aware of the situation and even encouraged it.

> WHY IT HURT SO MUCH:

Getting to the 1997 Final Four was a big deal for the university and for the whole state. It had never been done before in our team's history. This scandal tainted that team's legacy and our memories of it.

Bobby Jackson led our team to the 1997 Final Four.

> THE AFTERMATH:

Four players were immediately suspended and did not play in the 1999 tournament game. (The Gophers lost, 75-63.) Newby refused to testify and was fired. Haskins, athletic director Mark Deinhart, and university vice president McKinley Boston all eventually resigned. On October 24, 2000, our 1997 Final Four was vacated—so it never happened, according to the official record. The program was put on probation for four years.

#8: KIRBY PUCKETT RETIRES DUE TO LOSS OF VISION

 July 12, 1996   HEARTBREAK RATING: 💔💔💔💔💔

> WHAT HAPPENED:

In March 1996, Minnesota Twins all-star outfielder Kirby Puckett awakened one morning unable to see clearly out of his right eye. For the first time in his 12-year career, Puckett was placed on the disabled list (for injured players who cannot participate in games). Doctors could see there was fluid on his retina, but they were unsure how to fix the problem.

Puckett was diagnosed with a rare form of glaucoma, or increased pressure within the eyeball. He underwent three rounds of laser surgery to correct the problem, but none were successful. On July 12, he tried a fourth surgery. During that surgery, doctors found permanent damage to his retina. Later that day, Puckett announced his retirement from baseball.

> WHY IT HURT SO MUCH:

Puckett might be the greatest player ever to put on a Minnesota uniform—in any sport. Not only was he one of the best athletes, he was also a true leader. He reportedly told his teammates to "jump on [his] back" before Game 6 of the 1991 World Series because he would carry the team to victory. Then he made a spectacular game-saving catch against the center field

Kirby Puckett hit two home runs during the 1991 World Series.

wall. After that, he hit the game-winning, walk-off home run. It prompted legendary sports broadcaster Jack Buck to exclaim, "And we'll see you tomorrow night!"

> THE AFTERMATH:

After retiring, Puckett went on to work in the organization's front office. The Twins retired his jersey number (34) in 1997, and he was elected into the National Baseball Hall of Fame in 2001. The team struggled to replace him. It took six seasons after Puckett retired for Minnesota to finish with a winning record. Fans seemed to take just as long to find a new favorite player. The organization went so far as to implement a "Get to Know 'em" advertising campaign to help fans connect with the roster. This seemed to work, as Minnesota fell in love with players like Cristian Guzman, Torii Hunter, Corey Koskie, and Doug Mientkiewicz.

> DAN'S NOTES:

Kirby's retirement was a "where were you when . . . ?" moment for Minnesota sports fans. I watched the press conference in my parents' living room. Regardless of where you were, I think it's safe to say that we all cried together. I had reservations about including this entry because the book's goal is to be therapeutic and laugh about misfortune, but this one isn't funny. I, too, have lost some vision in my right eye due to retinal issues. Kirby was perhaps the most beloved Minnesota athlete of all time. His retirement was so heartbreaking for Minnesota sports fans that we had to include it.

#7A: NORTH STARS LOSE THE STANLEY CUP FINALS (1981)

May 21, 1981 HEARTBREAK RATING: ♥♥♥♥♥

> WHAT HAPPENED:

In 1981, the Minnesota North Stars were led by fan favorite forward Bobby Smith. It was the first season for Don Beaupre, Dino Ciccarelli, and Neal Broten (who played in three games). On February 26, we faced the Boston Bruins at Boston Garden. Seven seconds into the game, one of the most famous series of hockey fights in the history of the NHL began. All totaled, the two teams tallied an NHL-record 406 penalty minutes, and 12 players were ejected. Even though the North Stars lost the game, 5–1, the team sent a message to Boston that we wouldn't be pushed around. In the first round of the playoffs, the ninth-seeded North Stars matched up with the eighth-seeded Bruins. Minnesota swept the Bruins, winning three games to none. In the quarterfinals, the North Stars breezed past the fifth-seeded Buffalo Sabres, four games to one. In the semifinals, we ousted the Calgary Flames by winning four out of six games.

In the Stanley Cup Finals, the North Stars faced the defending champions and top overall seed, the New York Islanders. The Islanders showed their experience by jumping to a four-goal lead in Game 1. Ciccarelli put the North Stars on the scoreboard with a goal and an assist, but his team fell, 6–3. In Game 2,

Ciccarelli gave the North Stars an early lead, but the Islanders answered three times in the first period to take momentum back. The Islanders won again, 6–3. Minnesota meant business in Game 3. We jumped to a 3–1 lead in the first period. Unfortunately, the Islanders came back in the second period with three unanswered goals. The Islanders won, 7–5, led by a hat trick (three goals) from Butch Goring. The North Stars fought valiantly in Game 4, refusing to be swept. We defeated the Islanders, 4–2. In Game 5, however, New York closed out the series. They won the game, 5–1, and took home the Stanley Cup for the second year in a row.

> WHY IT HURT SO MUCH:

The North Stars had never won an NHL championship, and fate was on our side for most of the playoffs. We were underdogs in every series, yet we overachieved and went on an incredible run. It started to feel like destiny. So when the Stanley Cup eluded us, fans were devastated.

> THE AFTERMATH:

The North Stars were a young team, so it seemed likely that we would continue to contend. We finished first in the division in two of the next three seasons. We got as far as the conference finals in 1984 (page 58). As for the Islanders, they won the next two Stanley Cups, in 1982 and again in 1983, giving them four straight championships. It would've been nice of them to let us have the one.

The North Stars eliminated
the Chicago Blackhawks
from the 1991 playoffs.

#7B: NORTH STARS LOSE THE STANLEY CUP FINALS (1991)

 May 25, 1991 HEARTBREAK RATING:

> WHAT HAPPENED:

The 1991 NHL playoff bracket was grouped by division, meaning the Minnesota North Stars played teams in our own Norris Division for the first two rounds. This division included the two best teams in the entire league: the Chicago Blackhawks and the Saint Louis Blues. Minnesota eked into the playoffs with a losing record of 27–39–14. To say we were a long shot was an understatement. We matched up against the heavily favored Blackhawks in the division semifinals. The North Stars ended Chicago's season, four games to two. In the division finals, we upset the Blues in six games. We beat the defending-champion Edmonton Oilers in the conference finals, four games to one, to advance to the Stanley Cup Finals. There, we were pitted against the Pittsburgh Penguins.

The Minnesota magic continued in Game 1. The North Stars beat the Penguins, 5–4. We lost Game 2, but Game 3 looked promising. Minnesota was playing at home, at the Met Center. Plus, the Penguins' best player, Mario Lemieux, was out due to injury. The North Stars seized this chance and won the game, 3–1. Lemieux was back for Game 4, and he sparked the Penguins to three goals in the first few minutes. The North Stars fought back but ultimately lost, 5–3. In Game 5, Minnesota again dug a hole, falling behind 4–0. We staged a comeback but fell short, 6–4. Game 6 was a blowout: The North Stars were blanked, 8–0, in our last chance to stay alive in the series. It was a bitter end to an otherwise dreamlike run.

WHY IT HURT SO MUCH:

This truly was a Cinderella story. Nobody expected the North Stars to win the first series, let alone get so far. We were hot at the right time and upset higher-ranked teams, only to turn back into a pumpkin before midnight. In addition, this loss was near the end of the North Stars' time in Minnesota. We didn't know it then, but the team would only play two more seasons here.

THE AFTERMATH:

The previous year (1990), the North Stars had almost moved to San Jose, but hockey legend Lou Nanne negotiated a deal with the NHL: The North Stars' owners, brothers George and Gordon Gund, would get an expansion franchise—the San Jose Sharks—if a new owner could be found for Minnesota. On May 2, 1990, the Gunds agreed to sell the team. Part of the deal was that the roster would be divided between the North Stars and the Sharks. That "dividing" was officially called a dispersal draft; it occurred on May 30, 1991—just a few days after the Stanley Cup Finals.

DAN'S NOTES:

I remember watching the playoffs. Many fans, including my parents, were really upset that it was only on pay-per-view.

#6: DREW PEARSON'S PUSH-OFF ENDS THE VIKINGS' SEASON

 December 28, 1975   HEARTBREAK RATING: 💜💜💜💜💜

> WHAT HAPPENED:

The Minnesota Vikings squared off against the Dallas Cowboys in the 1975 NFC Divisional Playoffs. The Vikings were ahead, 14–10, with 44 seconds left. Dallas had the ball on their own 25-yard line. On fourth down, with 16 yards to go, Dallas quarterback Roger Staubach threw a pass to wide receiver Drew Pearson at midfield. Pearson caught the football near the Vikings' sideline, but it looked like he came down out of bounds. The referee ruled that Pearson would have come down in bounds, but Vikings defender Nate Wright had pushed him out. Dallas was awarded the reception, which gave them a first down. That set up the infamous "push-off" play. With about 30 seconds left, Staubach threw a deep pass to Pearson. The receiver appeared to push Wright out of his way in order to catch the ball. Wright fell to the ground, and Pearson ran into the end zone for the score. There were no penalty flags thrown, but fans threw oranges and a whiskey bottle at the referees. The Cowboys won, 17–14.

> WHY IT HURT SO MUCH:

The Vikings were favored in this game by eight points. Of all those legendary "Purple People Eaters" teams in the 1970s,

Drew Pearson scored the game-winning touchdown.

many experts believe that this team was the best of them and that we would have won the Super Bowl that year.

> THE AFTERMATH:

Staubach later claimed that he said a Hail Mary after throwing the pass. Thus, the football term "Hail Mary" (a desperation deep pass) was born. Pearson argued that he didn't push off. Dallas went on to play in the Super Bowl but lost to the Pittsburgh Steelers.

#5: THE MINNESOTA VIKINGS TRADE FOR HERSCHEL WALKER

 October 12, 1989   HEARTBREAK RATING: 🖤🖤🖤🖤🖤

 WHAT HAPPENED:

The Dallas Cowboys began the 1989 season 0–5. Head coach Jimmy Johnson wanted to rebuild and was looking to trade star running back Herschel Walker. Johnson's assistants tried to talk him out of it, but Johnson got in touch with Minnesota Vikings general manager Mike Lynn. The Vikings were 3–2, and Lynn believed Walker could help us win a Super Bowl. On October 12, the teams finalized a trade. Dallas received five players—Issiac Holt (CB), David Howard (LB), Darrin Nelson (RB), Jesse Solomon (LB), and Alex Stewart (DE)—along with Minnesota's first-round draft pick in 1992. Minnesota received Walker. Dallas fans and media were not happy. However, the trade was far from over.

Nelson refused to report to Dallas, so he was traded to San Diego. Johnson planned to cut the other players and receive more (conditional) picks from the Vikings. The coach claimed publicly that he had committed the "Great Train Robbery."

Lynn was stuck. He had to salvage as much of the situation as he could. On February 1, 1990, he and Johnson made another deal. Dallas kept Holt, Howard, Solomon, and the conditional picks, but they gave the Vikings some draft picks in return. All together, Minnesota ended up with Dallas's third- and tenth-round picks in 1990, San Diego's fifth-round pick in 1990, and Dallas's third-round pick in 1991. The Cowboys got Minnesota's first-, second-, and sixth-round picks in 1990; Minnesota's first- and second-round picks in 1991; and Minnesota's first-, second-, and third-round picks in 1992. It was the largest player trade in NFL history.

> WHY IT HURT SO MUCH:

We mortgaged our team's future success for a player who was supposed to lead us to a Super Bowl. Instead, with Walker on the roster, our team was 21–23, including a playoff loss. This occurred after the Drew Pearson push-off (page 32) and before the North Stars moved (page 36). Minnesota seems to have an unhealthy cosmic sports connection to Dallas.

> THE AFTERMATH:

While we floundered, Dallas drafted players like Emmitt Smith (RB), Russell Maryland (DT), and Darren Woodson (S). The Vikings released Walker in May 1992 after failing to trade him. He signed with Philadelphia. That same season, the Cowboys won their first of three Super Bowls in the 1990s.

> DAN'S NOTES:

I remember Herschel's first game, literally watching him run out of his shoe on his way to 148 yards. I also remember thinking, "We're gonna win it all." Unfortunately, that was Herschel's best game as a Viking.

#4: THE MINNESOTA NORTH STARS GET MOVED TO DALLAS

 March 10, 1993   HEARTBREAK RATING:

> WHAT HAPPENED:

The Minnesota North Stars played at the Met Center, but the team didn't own the arena. They were tenants. The Metropolitan Sports Facilities Commission (MSFC) owned the facility. The Met Center needed renovations for the team to compete in the modern financial world of the NHL. The North Stars requested improvements on many occasions and were willing to pay for some of them. The team was repeatedly denied. The MSFC wanted the North Stars to move to a facility downtown—which wouldn't have been any better for the team, financially. On January 30, 1990, the owners (George and Gordon Gund) asked one last time for improvements and were denied.

On May 2, 1990, the North Stars were sold to Howard Baldwin and Morris Belzberg. A month later, Norm Green bought a controlling interest in the team. He took over as team president when Baldwin resigned in July. Unfortunately, Green ran into the same MSFC stonewall that the Gunds had encountered. With no hope for getting a competitive facility in Minnesota, Green made the decision to move the franchise to Dallas. The devastating news was made public on March 10, 1993.

> WHY IT HURT SO MUCH:

Minnesota is known as the "State of Hockey." The sport is arguably more popular here than anywhere else in the country, and Minnesotans loved our North Stars. Even before 1993, the team almost left several times—only to be saved at the last minute. This time, nobody came to the rescue. Worse yet, the person who fans thought would keep the team here instead sent the North Stars away forever.

> THE AFTERMATH:

Almost immediately, public officials began trying to attract another NHL franchise to Minnesota. There were reports that the Oilers, Jets, and Whalers were interested in moving. None of them came. In 1997, Minnesota was granted an expansion franchise. It cost significantly more than it would have to keep the North Stars and pay for the requested renovations. The Dallas Stars won the Stanley Cup in 1999 (page 69).

> DAN'S NOTES:

It's great to have hockey back, but when the North Stars left, they took a piece of me with them. It's never felt the same. The North Stars have been gone longer than they were here. I bet fans who have only known the Wild in their lifetime love them as much as I loved the North Stars.

Side Note: When Dallas was courting the North Stars, there were reports that Dallas Cowboys legend Roger Staubach showed Green around the city. Rumor had it that Green displayed an autographed football from Staubach in his office.

#3A: THE MINNESOTA VIKINGS LOSE SUPER BOWL IV (1970)

 January 11, 1970   HEARTBREAK RATING: ♥♥♥♥♥

> WHAT HAPPENED:

In 1970, professional football was not as we know it today. There were two different leagues: the National Football League (NFL) and the American Football League (AFL). The Minnesota Vikings (12–2) were champions of the NFL. The Super Bowl pitted us against the AFL's Kansas City Chiefs, who touted a record of 11–3 but didn't win their division in the regular season. The NFL was considered a superior league, so the Vikings were favored to beat the Chiefs by 12 points.

In a sign of things to come, a Vikings mascot had a mishap during the Super Bowl's pregame ceremony. A hot-air balloon carrying a man dressed as a Viking was trying to take off from midfield. The balloon got caught in a wind gust. It ended up in the stands and nearly injured several people.

Minnesota's strength was our defense, led by future hall-of-famers Carl Eller, Alan Page, and Paul Krause. The defense's front four were nicknamed the Purple People Eaters. However, Kansas City coach Hank Stram's creativity on offense kept the Vikings defense off-balance. The Chiefs jumped to an early lead, scoring field goals by Jan Stenerud (48 and 32 yards) on two of their first three drives. In the second quarter, Stenerud added a 25-yard field goal. The Vikings fumbled the ensuing kickoff, and it was recovered by the Chiefs. That turned into a five-yard touchdown run by Mike Garrett. The Chiefs led 16–0 at halftime. The Vikings' only score came on the first drive of the third quarter, when Dave Osborn scored on a four-yard run. The Chiefs answered with a 46-yard touchdown pass from Len Dawson to Otis Taylor on their next possession. In the fourth quarter, with the score at 23–7, the Chiefs intercepted the Vikings three times to put away the game.

> WHY IT HURT SO MUCH:

This is considered one of the greatest upsets in NFL history. The Chiefs defense included some former Minnesota Golden Gophers—particularly future hall-of-famer Bobby Bell (DE/LB). They held the Vikings' running game to 67 yards. Minnesota quarterback Joe Kapp said after the game that the Kansas City defenders "looked like a redwood forest."

> THE AFTERMATH:

This was the final year of the AFL and, thus, the last Super Bowl between the AFL and the NFL. The two leagues merged in 1970. The Chiefs didn't win another Super Bowl until 2020. The Vikings finished first in the NFC Central Division the next two seasons. We lost in the divisional round both years: to the San Francisco 49ers in 1970 and to the Dallas Cowboys in 1971.

#3B: THE MINNESOTA VIKINGS LOSE SUPER BOWL VIII (1974)

 January 13, 1974   HEARTBREAK RATING:

> WHAT HAPPENED:

The Miami Dolphins were riding high. They had played in the previous two Super Bowls and had won Super Bowl VII the year before. They finished the 1973 regular season with the best record in the AFC at 12–2. The Dolphins beat the Cincinnati Bengals, 34–16, in the divisional round of the playoffs, and they defeated the Oakland Raiders, 27–10, in the AFC Championship. The Minnesota Vikings were also 12–2. We defeated the Washington Redskins, 27–20, in the divisional round and then the Dallas Cowboys, 27–10, in the NFC Championship. The Dolphins defense had given up the fewest points in the league, and Miami was favored to win Super Bowl VIII by 6.5 points.

Miami scored twice in the first quarter: on a five-yard Larry Csonka run and then on a one-yard Jim Kiick plunge. The Dolphins added a Garo Yepremian field goal in the second quarter to go up 17–0. Minnesota tried to stage a comeback. With just under a minute left in the half, we advanced to the Dolphins' six-yard line. On fourth down with a yard to go, Vikings running back Oscar Reed took the handoff from Fran Tarkenton. Reed was hit by Dolphins linebacker Nick Buoniconti

and fumbled. The Dolphins' Jake Scott jumped on the football, securing the turnover. The Vikings never seemed to bounce back.

In the third quarter Csonka scored again—giving Miami a 24–0 advantage. The Vikings finally got on the board early in the fourth quarter when Tarkenton rushed into the end zone from four yards out. A few minutes later, the Vikings got going again. With just under seven minutes left, Minnesota faced third down at the Miami 32-yard line. Tarkenton threw a deep pass to receiver Jim Lash. It was intercepted, sealing defeat for the purple and gold.

> WHY IT HURT SO MUCH:

This was a beatdown. The Vikings could not stop the Dolphins' rushing attack. Miami ran for 196 yards, with Csonka gaining 145. Miami quarterback Bob Griese only threw seven passes in the game. Plus, for as good as the Vikings defense was, the Dolphins defense was better. (Their 1973 defense is widely considered one of the best of all time.) We couldn't find the end zone in Super Bowl VIII, and Miami ran right through us.

> THE AFTERMATH:

Csonka was the first running back to be named the MVP of a Super Bowl. The Dolphins returned to the big game in 1983 and 1985, but they lost both times. The Vikings returned to the Super Bowl in 1975 (page 44) and 1977 (page 46).

The Purple People Eaters: Jim Marshall, Gary Larsen, Carl Eller, and Alan Page.

#3C: THE MINNESOTA VIKINGS LOSE SUPER BOWL IX (1975)

 January 12, 1975   HEARTBREAK RATING: ♥♥♥♥♥

> WHAT HAPPENED:

The Minnesota Vikings finished the 1974 regular season with a record of 10–4. The Pittsburgh Steelers entered the playoffs with a comparable 10–3–1 record. Not only was 1975 the Steelers' first Super Bowl, it was also just their fourth playoff appearance in more than 40 seasons.

The game began ugly. The Steelers botched two field goal attempts, and the Vikings missed one. In the second quarter, Minnesota had the ball deep in our own territory. A failed handoff exchange between quarterback Fran Tarkenton and running back Dave Osborn resulted in the football rolling into the end zone. Tarkenton chased the ball down and fell on it, resulting in a safety. The Vikings rallied with a drive all the way to Pittsburgh's 25-yard line. Tarkenton zipped a pass to receiver John Gilliam at the five-yard line, but it was tipped into the air and intercepted by Mel Blount. The half ended with the Steelers ahead, 2–0.

The second half began with the Vikings fumbling a line-drive kickoff that skidded across the wet turf. Pittsburgh recovered. Four plays later, running back Franco Harris scored the game's first touchdown on a nine-yard run. In the fourth quarter, Vikings safety Paul Krause recovered a Harris fumble near midfield. A pass interference penalty gave Minnesota the ball at the five-yard line. But running back Chuck Foreman fumbled, and the ball was recovered by Steelers legend Joe Greene. Four plays later, the Steelers were forced to punt. It was blocked by Vikings linebacker Matt Blair and recovered in the end zone by Terry Brown for a touchdown. A missed extra point cut Minnesota's deficit to 9–6 with 11 minutes left in the game. The Steelers' next drive ate up seven minutes and ended in a Larry Brown touchdown reception from Terry Bradshaw. On Minnesota's next possession, Tarkenton was intercepted for the third time, effectively ending the game at the score of 16–6.

> WHY IT HURT SO MUCH:

This game was close until the final minutes, and it could have gone either way. The field was wet, and the Vikings continually thwarted our opportunities with turnovers. In addition, the Steelers defense held the Vikings' running game to 17 yards on 21 carries, which at the time was the worst single-game rushing total in Vikings history.

> THE AFTERMATH:

It was the first of four Super Bowl wins for Pittsburgh's "Steel Curtain" dynasty of the 1970s. In 1975, the Vikings finished 12–2 but missed the Super Bowl (page 32). Tarkenton was named the league's MVP of the 1975 season.

#3D: THE MINNESOTA VIKINGS LOSE SUPER BOWL XI (1977)

 January 9, 1977   HEARTBREAK RATING: ♥♥♥♥♥

> WHAT HAPPENED:

In 1976, the Oakland Raiders finished the regular season with the best record in the league at 13–1. The Minnesota Vikings held a mark of 11–2–1. The Raiders were favored in the Super Bowl by four points.

In the first quarter, the Vikings' Fred McNeill blocked a punt and recovered it at the Oakland three-yard line. Two plays later, a fumble gave the ball back to the Raiders. They drove down the field and converted a 24-yard field goal. That seemed to awaken the Raiders' offense. They scored on their next two drives, first on a one-yard pass from quarterback Ken Stabler to tight end Dave Casper and then on a one-yard run by Pete Banaszak. At halftime, Oakland held a 16–0 lead.

In the third quarter, the Raiders added another field goal before the Vikings offense showed any signs of life. With just over a minute left in the third, receiver Sammy White caught an eight-yard touchdown reception from quarterback Fran Tarkenton. (It would be the only touchdown pass he ever threw in a Super Bowl.) In the fourth quarter, Tarkenton threw a pass that was intercepted by cornerback Willie Hall. That led to another Banaszak touchdown run with about eight minutes to go. Sensing the clock ticking away, the Vikings came out passing. We quickly moved the ball into Raiders territory. From Oakland's 28-yard line, Tarkenton threw a short pass that was again intercepted by Brown. He returned it 75 yards for a touchdown. Tarkenton was benched, and he watched his team score a meaningless touchdown in the game's final minute. Oakland dominated, 32–14, and they set a Super Bowl record for most offensive yards gained by a team (429).

> WHY IT HURT SO MUCH:

Minnesota was the first team to lose four Super Bowls, and those Vikings teams were some of the best in NFL history. We were led by seven future hall-of-famers. The team was so good for so long; it's sad that we don't have a championship to show for it. Getting that close that many times and coming up short is almost as unlikely as getting there and winning.

> THE AFTERMATH:

Vikings head coach Bud Grant said after the game, "We just played them on the wrong day. Next time we'll play them on a Wednesday." The Vikings did not return to the Super Bowl. Those four losses still seem to be a giant monkey on our collective backs. It's like a curse that continues to haunt us.

> DAN'S NOTES:

I still have the #44 Chuck Foreman jersey that I wore as a kid (page 256). I like to joke with my parents to thank/blame them for turning me into a Minnesota sports fan.

#2: NFC CHAMPIONSHIP: MINNESOTA VS. NEW ORLEANS

 January 24, 2010   HEARTBREAK RATING: ♥♥♥♥♥

> WHAT HAPPENED:

With the game tied, 28–28, late in the fourth quarter, the Minnesota Vikings took possession of the football. We methodically drove all the way to the New Orleans Saints' 33-yard line. With just 19 seconds left on the clock, the team was poised to kick a game-winning field goal. But after taking a timeout, Minnesota was flagged for too many men in the huddle. That five-yard penalty pushed us out of kicker Ryan Longwell's range. On the next play, quarterback Brett Favre made an ill-advised throw across his body that was intercepted. The game went into overtime, and the Vikings never got the ball. The Saints kicked a field goal on their opening possession and won.

> WHY IT HURT SO MUCH:

The 2009 season felt magical from the start. It began in August when Favre chose to join the Vikings. Minnesota became a "team of destiny" in Week 3: Favre completed an incredible 32-yard touchdown pass with two seconds on the clock to defeat the San Francisco 49ers. Even the most grizzled Vikings fan felt the season was different. Week after week, everything seemed to be going our way, so a lot of us let ourselves believe again.

> THE AFTERMATH:

Many fans who watched the game got a sense that something was amiss. It turned out we were right. The Saints went on to win the Super Bowl—*our* Super Bowl. However, in the offseason, it was reported that New Orleans had implemented an illegal "bounty" program. Players would apparently receive bonus money for injuring key Vikings players. (Favre was injured in the game, although he played till the end.) Saints head coach Sean Payton and defensive coordinator Gregg Williams were both suspended the following season. The NFL changed its overtime rules in March 2010: Unless the opening drive results in a touchdown, both teams get a chance to score. Favre returned to the Vikings for the 2010 season, but the magic was gone. The team failed to make the playoffs, and Favre retired.

> DAN'S NOTES:

This was one of my favorite Vikings seasons. I had a man-crush on Favre and was back to bleeding purple. After the championship game, I felt as if I had been dumped. I still haven't been able to re-watch the game. Some blame Favre for the loss, but without him, we wouldn't have been there. Besides, I share some of the blame too. I hadn't washed my Favre jersey all season. But I washed it before this game; I had to wear it to work. As for that "12-men" penalty, head coach Brad Childress blamed himself. He changed the personnel at the last second, and at least one player was not informed.

#1: NFC CHAMPIONSHIP: ATLANTA VS. MINNESOTA

 January 17, 1999   HEARTBREAK RATING:

WHAT HAPPENED:

The Minnesota Vikings' 1998 team was the best since the Purple People Eaters of the 1970s (pages 38–45). Minnesota went 15–1 in the regular season and secured home-field advantage throughout the NFC playoffs. We walloped the Arizona Cardinals in the divisional round, 41–21. That brought the Atlanta Falcons to Minneapolis for the NFC Championship Game. The Vikings were favored to win by 11 points.

Minnesota led 20–7 in the second quarter, and it seemed as if the rout was on. But Atlanta scored a touchdown with 59 seconds left in the half, cutting the Vikings' lead to six points. The pesky Falcons kept it close after that. The Vikings were ahead, 27–20, with 6:07 to go in the game. After stopping the Falcons on fourth down, Minnesota began a drive from our own 25-yard line. The offense ate up nearly four minutes and moved the ball to Atlanta's 21-yard line. A field goal would give the Vikings a 10-point lead without enough time for the Falcons to rally. Kicker Gary Anderson came into the game for a 38-yard attempt. Just before the snap, television analyst Pat Summerall said, "Anderson hasn't missed in two years." The kick went wide left. The Vikings maintained a seven-point edge.

The Falcons took over with 2:07 remaining. On that drive, quarterback Chris Chandler threw a pass that Vikings safety Robert Griffith could have intercepted, but the ball fell to the ground. On the next play, Atlanta scored the tying touchdown. The Vikings got the football back with 49 seconds on the clock. On third down and three yards to go, with 30 seconds and two timeouts left, the Vikings chose to let time run out. Quarterback Randall Cunningham kneeled down, and the game went into overtime. The Falcons kicked a field goal and won, 30–27.

> WHY IT HURT SO MUCH:

Anderson had been perfect on field goals and extra points for the entire season. In addition, the Vikings had one of the best offenses in the history of the NFL. We set the record for most points scored in a season. Yet we took a knee . . . to play for overtime. It's a decision that still haunts fans.

> THE AFTERMATH:

This game was the beginning of our modern era of field goal follies. From Doug Brien to Blair Walsh (page 173) to Daniel Carlson (page 176), our kickers and the field goals they've missed have become an infamous part of Vikings lore.

> DAN'S NOTES:

Prior to the game, I joked with friends, "What if Gary Anderson misses one?" I'm not sure why I said it. Even then, I was superstitious—and a Vikings fatalist. I know it's ridiculous, but somehow, I still feel like that missed kick was my fault.

CHAPTER 2
SKATING ON THIN ICE

On February 9, 1966, Minnesota was awarded a new NHL franchise. The team was named the North Stars on May 25. Ground was broken for the new arena, the Metropolitan Sports Center (aka the Met Center) on October 3. We played our first game there on October 21, 1967, and we won our first ever game that night, beating the California Seals, 3–1, in front of a crowd of 12,951. I spent a lot of time at the Met Center over the years; a family friend brought me to quite a few games. I remember how raucous the crowd could get, especially when we played the Chicago Blackhawks. I smile about all the memories, but they carry a bit of sadness too. When the North Stars left (page 36), it impacted me—and so many other fans. Of course, that isn't the only infamous hockey event in our state's history.

FIGHTING SAINTS WHA TEAM QUITS IN AN AIRPORT LOBBY

 February 28, 1976 HEARTBREAK RATING:

WHAT HAPPENED:

In 1971, the World Hockey Association (WHA) was formed. The Minnesota Fighting Saints were among the 10 franchises that began play in the league's 1972 inaugural season. The team started out in the Saint Paul Auditorium (now Roy Wilkins Auditorium) but moved to the Saint Paul Civic Center when it opened in January 1973. Some colorful characters were on the team. The Carlson brothers (Jack, Jeff, and Steve) were the inspiration for the Hanson brothers in the film *Slap Shot*. (Steve and Jeff acted in it.) Another *Slap Shot* character, Ogie Oglethorpe, was inspired by Bill "Goldie" Goldthorpe, who was with the Fighting Saints for the 1973–1974 season. He was called the "wildest, meanest, most unpredictable player in hockey."

Several teams in the WHA—including the Saints—struggled financially because they tried to offer higher salaries to entice players away from the NHL. By late February 1976, the Saints could not afford to pay the players. The owners tried to sell the team but couldn't find the right offer. On February 28, the team was scheduled to fly to Cincinnati, Ohio, to play against the Stingers. The players were frustrated that they hadn't received their last few paychecks. Some didn't even bother coming to the Minneapolis-Saint Paul International Airport. Those who did show up voted to quit the team. A group of 50 Fighting Saints booster club members had taken a bus trip to Cincinnati. They ended up watching the Houston Aeros replace the Saints in the game. The diehard fans "drowned [their] sorrows," according to the club president.

> WHY IT HURT SO MUCH:

The first Fighting Saints squad played in four seasons, and we made the playoffs every year. The Saints tried to roster local players, which appealed to many Minnesotans.

> THE AFTERMATH:

Plagued by financial difficulties, many WHA teams folded or moved. On August 9, 1976, the Cleveland Crusaders came to Minnesota and became the new Fighting Saints. That team folded on January 20, 1977. By 1979, only seven teams remained. The WHA negotiated a merger with the NHL, which accepted four of the teams into the league: the Edmonton Oilers, Hartford Whalers, Quebec Nordiques, and Winnipeg Jets.

> SIDE NOTES:

By 1976, the NHL's California Seals were experiencing financial difficulties. The team's minority owners George and Gordon Gund were originally from Cleveland, so the franchise moved there and became the Cleveland Barons. (This led to the Crusaders coming to Minnesota, as mentioned above.) In 1978, the Barons merged with the Minnesota North Stars, and the Gunds took over ownership of the team.

Minnesota's original Fighting Saints
played in the WHA from 1972 to 1976.

EDMONTON SWEEPS NORTH STARS IN CONFERENCE FINALS

 May 1, 1984   HEARTBREAK RATING:

> WHAT HAPPENED:

The early 1980s were some of the Minnesota North Stars' best years. In the 1983–1984 season, the North Stars finished the regular season first in the Norris Division (39–31–10; 88 points). We beat the Chicago Blackhawks in the first round, three games to two. We beat the Saint Louis Blues, four games to three in the division finals (winning an overtime thriller in Game 7). Then the North Stars advanced to play the Edmonton Oilers in the conference finals. The Oilers had seven future hall-of-famers: Glenn Anderson, Paul Coffey, Grant Fuhr, Wayne Gretzky, Jarri Kurri, Mark Messier, and coach Glen Sather. Edmonton set a record that year for the most goals scored in an 80-game season (446). Gretzky had 87 of those himself.

The first two games were in Edmonton. True to their reputation, the Oilers came out firing. Edmonton won the first game, 7–1. In Game 2, the Oilers jumped ahead, 2–0, in the first. Minnesota fought back in the second period with goals from Neal Broten and Willie Plett. After Edmonton struck again, Brian Bellows tied the game, 3–3. At one point, Oilers owner Peter Pocklington said to North Stars owner George Gund, "Maybe we'll let this series get to five games." But Gretzky scored the game-winning goal in the third period. (There was some controversy as to whether Gretzky had actually scored, but it was ruled a goal.) The next two games were back at the Met Center. In Game 3, the North Stars scored an eye-popping five straight goals in the second period (four of them on power plays). Not to be outdone, Edmonton answered with five goals in the third period. The Oilers won, 8–5. In much quieter fashion, Edmonton won Game 4—and a trip to the Stanley Cup Finals—by a score of 3–1.

> WHY IT HURT SO MUCH:

After having a great run of successful seasons, it felt like we were due in 1984. But running into a team of destiny like the Oilers (in the first year of their dynasty) was just bad luck. Not only did Minnesota get swept, we were outscored, 22–10.

> THE AFTERMATH:

Minnesota general manager Lou Nanne said, ". . . when we ran into Edmonton it was like running into a buzz saw." The Oilers won their first Stanley Cup that year. Edmonton's dynasty ultimately claimed four of the next six championships. They were the only team in history to score more than 400 goals in a season—and they did it five times during the 1980s.

> DAN'S NOTES:

Nanne acquired the first overall draft pick in 1983 via a trade. With that pick, we selected Brian Lawton (266 career points) ahead of future hall-of-famers Steve Yzerman (1,755 points), Pat LaFontaine (1,013 points), and Cam Neely (694 points).

DINO CICCARELLI RUNS INTO LEGAL TROUBLES

1987–1988

HEARTBREAK RATING:

> WHAT HAPPENED:

In 1987, Minnesota North Stars forward Dino Ciccarelli was not only one of the team's most popular players but was probably also our best. However, a neighbor of his in Eden Prairie, Minnesota, reported to police on four separate occasions that Ciccarelli had been outside without clothes. On November 25, police watched Ciccarelli from a nearby house. They took photos of him in his front yard wearing a sweatshirt—and nothing else. He was arrested for misdemeanor indecent exposure. Ciccarelli said he was sick in a bathroom when he heard a noise and went to investigate. He said that he only stepped a foot or two from the doorway and immediately went back inside. He also issued a statement through his lawyer that said he had "never at any time set one foot outside [his] house without being covered from the waist down." He was formally charged on November 30. Ciccarelli initially pled not guilty.

On January 6, 1988, Ciccarelli got into a scrap during a game in Toronto. He swung his stick and hit the Maple Leafs' Luke Richardson in the head and neck. Ciccarelli argued that he was small and wasn't a good fighter. He also felt that Richardson raised his stick first, so he was just defending himself.

In response to the incident, Toronto authorities issued a warrant for his arrest on January 8. Ciccarelli was charged with assault. He pled not guilty and claimed self-defense. On January 20, he pled guilty to the indecent exposure charge. He was ordered to attend counseling and pay court costs. On August 24, he was found guilty on the assault charge in a Toronto court. He was sentenced to a day in jail and a $1,000 fine. He speculated that the court and the NHL were trying to make an example of him because no NHL player had ever before received jail time for an on-ice incident.

> WHY IT HURT SO MUCH:

The 1987–1988 season was one of the worst in North Stars history (page 62). The "no pants" report was a shocking moment in the midst of it. It led to unsubstantiated rumors, speculation, and urban legends. Ciccarelli was suspended by the league for 10 games during an injury-riddled season. The North Stars finished the season with a 19–48–13 record (51 points), the worst record in the league. Despite the 10-game suspension, Ciccarelli led the team with 86 points.

> THE AFTERMATH:

Apparently, no one from the North Stars organization picked up Ciccarelli from jail in 1988. He reportedly had to ride with a reporter to his hotel. This contributed to a contract dispute ahead of the 1988 season; Ciccarelli held out until October 3 before agreeing to a new contract. He was traded to the Washington Capitals in March 1989. He played for 10 more years and was elected to the Hockey Hall of Fame in 2010.

HERB BROOKS FIRED AFTER A SEASON WITH NORTH STARS

 June 22, 1988   HEARTBREAK RATING:

> WHAT HAPPENED:

Minnesota North Stars general manager Lou Nanne hired coach Herb Brooks ahead of the 1987–1988 season. In Brooks' first and only season, the North Stars finished with the worst record in the NHL and one of the worst records in team history. We suffered the most minutes missed due to injury in the history of the franchise. Add the distraction of Dino Ciccarelli's legal troubles (page 60) into the mix, and you can understand why the season was such a disappointment. Nanne became team president, and Jack Ferreira took over as the general manager. The relationships Brooks had with Ferreira and the team's owners were said to be tense. On June 22, 1988, the North Stars announced that Brooks would not be returning. According to the *Star Tribune*, the coach said that he found it interesting he was not being considered for a position he wasn't interested in and never applied for.

> WHY IT HURT SO MUCH:

Herb Brooks was—and still is—a Minnesota hockey legend. As a player, he won a state championship at Saint Paul Johnson High School. He went on to play for the Minnesota Golden Gophers and the U.S. Men's Olympic Team. He coached the

Herb Brooks coached the 1980 "Miracle on Ice" team.

Gophers to three NCAA championships and, most famously, coached the 1980 U.S. "miracle" hockey team to Olympic Gold. He was one of us, and the North Stars were our team. The fact that the two things couldn't coexist was a shame.

> THE AFTERMATH:

Brooks went on to coach the NHL's New Jersey Devils and Pittsburgh Penguins. In 2002, he also coached the U.S. Men's Olympic Team to a silver medal in Salt Lake City, Utah, before his tragic death the following year.

THE NORTH STARS PLAY IN THE TEAM'S FINAL HOME GAME

 April 13, 1993   HEARTBREAK RATING: ♥♥♥♥♥

> WHAT HAPPENED:

In March 1993, Norm Green announced that he would be moving the Minnesota North Stars to Dallas (page 36). That designated Tuesday, April 13, as the North Stars' final home game . . . *ever*. Fans gathered in the parking lot, tailgating and mourning the loss of our beloved franchise. Local and national media came to document the solemn event.

A sold-out crowd of faithful fans packed the Met Center to pay tribute, and they gave their favorite team a four-minute standing ovation. That was before Jim Bowers sang the national anthem. The North Stars lost the game, 3–2, to the Chicago Blackhawks, but the season wasn't over. Minnesota was still in the playoff hunt and had a game in Detroit two days later. We lost that final game to the Red Wings, 5–3, which eliminated the North Stars from playoff contention and put the final nail in the Minnesota team's coffin.

> WHY IT HURT SO MUCH:

The announcement that the team would be moving was the obituary. The visitation was held in the parking lot. The game was the funeral. The entire spectacle made it clear that, regardless of how much emotion and energy fans put into the local teams, we had no say in what happened to them.

> THE AFTERMATH:

The Met Center was imploded on December 13, 1994. The initial detonations left part of the structure standing, and some fans felt that was one last act of defiance against those who were responsible for moving the team. The franchise became the Dallas Stars. In 1999, the Stars won the Stanley Cup (page 69). A year later, they lost in the Stanley Cup Finals. Minnesota was without NHL hockey until we received an expansion franchise in 1997. Our new team, the Minnesota Wild, began play in 2000. The Xcel Energy Center was built in the late 1990s on the ground where the Saint Paul Civic Center once stood. It became home ice for the Wild. The expansion franchise and the new arena cost Minnesota substantially more than it would have to keep the North Stars here.

> DAN'S NOTES:

When the team left, some of us never got closure. The part I struggle with most as a fan is why we didn't fight to keep the name "North Stars"—much like Cleveland did when their NFL franchise, the Browns, became the Baltimore Ravens in 1996.

Side Note: The North Stars' last goal at the Met Center came from Russ Courtnall with 23 seconds left versus Chicago. The final goal in North Stars history was scored by Ulf Dahlen with 49 seconds to go in the game against Detroit.

Mike Modano played for both Minnesota and Dallas.

DALLAS PLAYS AN EXHIBITION GAME AT TARGET CENTER

 December 9, 1993   HEARTBREAK RATING:

 > WHAT HAPPENED:

The owners of the NBA's Minnesota Timberwolves, Marv Wolfenson and Harvey Ratner, were hoping to have the Minnesota North Stars as tenants at Target Center, which would help them pay off their debt. When the North Stars left, the two owners started looking for another NHL team to move to the Twin Cities and become a renter. They reached out to NHL commissioner Gary Bettman for help. To get a feel for Minnesota's interest in the return of the NHL, six exhibition games (called the Target Center Series) were scheduled: two NHL preseason games; two games featuring the U.S. Men's Olympic Hockey Team, one versus the Minnesota Gophers and one against Canada; and two regular-season NHL games.

Attendance for the series was disappointing. The largest crowd attended a regular-season game between the Dallas Stars and the Ottawa Senators. The official attendance was 14,058, which would be comparable to a North Stars game. However, media estimates put the actual attendance at thousands fewer. Those who did attend were heard chanting "Norm Sucks" throughout the night. (Stars owner Norm Green was attending the NHL Board of Governors meetings in California.) Dallas won, 6–1.

Former North Stars Mike Modano and Dave Gagner each scored two goals in the game.

> WHY IT HURT SO MUCH:

Before the North Stars left, the team's jerseys were redesigned to say "Stars." Some speculated this was done knowing that Green would be moving the team. At the exhibition game, those jerseys said "Dallas" and featured a patch in the shape of Texas. To many fans, that felt as if the league was parading our old team and some of our favorite players in front of us.

> THE AFTERMATH:

At that Board of Governors meeting on December 9, 1993, Edmonton Oilers owner Peter Pocklington updated the other owners on his intentions to move his team to Minnesota—and his legal battle over an injunction that prevented him from negotiating the relocation. The following summer, he reached an agreement to keep the Oilers in Edmonton. In October 1995, Richard Burke and Steven Gluckstern purchased the Winnipeg Jets and were interested in moving them to Minnesota. Instead, the team moved to Phoenix and became the Coyotes. Wolfenson and Ratner were left with no NHL team for Target Center (page 86).

> DAN'S NOTES:

I imagine that some marketing genius thought Minnesota fans would love to see our old team again—that we'd come out in droves. But this was salt in the wounds. It had been less than eight months since the "funeral" for the team (page 64).

THE DALLAS STARS WIN THE STANLEY CUP IN 1999

 June 19, 1999   HEARTBREAK RATING:

> WHAT HAPPENED:

After leaving Minnesota and becoming the Dallas Stars, our former team made the playoffs in four of their first five seasons and finished first in their division twice. They advanced as far as the Western Conference Finals in 1998, where they lost to the eventual Stanley Cup champions, the Detroit Red Wings, four games to two. The following season, Dallas finished first in their division again and won the Western Conference Finals over the Colorado Avalanche in seven games.

They advanced to the finals and defeated the Buffalo Sabres, four games to two, to win the first Stanley Cup in franchise history. Six former North Stars were on the team, four of whom played in the North Stars' final season in 1993 (page 36): Derian Hatcher, Craig Ludwig, Richard Matvichuk, and Mike Modano. Modano led the team in the playoffs with 23 points (five goals and 18 assists.)

> WHY IT HURT SO MUCH:

When Dallas came back for an exhibition game (page 67) it was painful to watch. This was piling on. Minnesota had been granted an NHL expansion franchise (the Wild in 1997), but the

team had not yet begun to play. So we watched the Dallas Stars with envy and even some bitterness. Our former team—and some of our former players—won a championship . . . without us. Although Norm Green had sold the Dallas Stars in 1996, he was given a championship ring by new owner Tom Hicks.

> THE AFTERMATH:

Dallas finished first in their division again the following year. They again advanced to the Stanley Cup Finals but lost to the New Jersey Devils in six games. The Wild and the Stars played against each other for the first time on December 17, 2000, at Xcel Energy Center in Saint Paul. The Wild won, 6–0.

Modano, who was drafted by the North Stars and played in Minnesota for four years, spent 16 seasons with Dallas. Coincidentally, his final game with Dallas was played against the Wild at Xcel Energy Center. After the game, Modano put on a North Stars jersey and skated back onto the ice to wave goodbye to the Minnesota fans. Modano retired in 2011 and was elected to the Hockey Hall of Fame in 2014. He was hired by the Minnesota Wild as an executive advisor.

> DAN'S NOTES:

I recently discovered an old Dallas Stars jersey packed away in some of my wife's old things from before we were married. We're working through it.

THE WILD LOSE CONFERENCE FINALS, SCORING JUST ONCE

 May 16, 2003 HEARTBREAK RATING:

> WHAT HAPPENED:

The NHL granted Minnesota an expansion franchise on June 25, 1997. On January 22, 1998, the team was named the Minnesota Wild. On June 24, 2000, the Wild drafted our first player: Marian Gaborik from Slovakia. Coached by hall-of-famer Jacques Lemaire, our team played its first game on October 6, 2000, and lost on the road to the Mighty Ducks of Anaheim. In that game, Gaborik scored the first goal in franchise history.

In the Wild's first two seasons, we finished in last place in our division. In our third season, led by Gaborik's 65 points, Minnesota finished in third place in the division and qualified for the playoffs as a sixth-seeded team. In the first round, we faced off against the heavily favored Colorado Avalanche. It was an incredible seven-game series in which the Wild won the last two games—both in overtime—to clinch the series. In the second round, we matched up with the Vancouver Canucks. This series also went seven games, and Minnesota again came out on top.

That led to the Western Conference Finals and a matchup with the Mighty Ducks. Game 1 went into overtime, scoreless. Eight

Marian Gaborik was the Wild's first ever draft pick.

minutes into a *second* overtime, the Ducks' Petr Sykora scored, winning the first game of the series. In Game 2, the Wild were blanked again, 2–0. The next two games were on the road at the Arrowhead Pond of Anaheim, California. The Wild failed to score in Game 3 and lost, 4–0. Facing elimination, the Wild's Andrew Brunette scored the team's only goal of the series, four minutes into Game 4, on a power play. The Ducks' Adam Oates answered twice, giving the Ducks the victory and a sweep of the series.

> WHY IT HURT SO MUCH:

This was the Wild's third season—and the first time we made the playoffs. Nobody expected us to do so well so soon. We were underdogs in every series, and the excitement of those first two rounds stirred up emotions in even the most bitter North Stars fans. After allowing ourselves to feel those emotions again, getting swept (and almost shut out) was a huge letdown.

> THE AFTERMATH:

The Mighty Ducks lost the Stanley Cup Finals to the New Jersey Devils in seven games. Over the next eight seasons, the Wild made the playoffs twice and lost in the first round both times.

PARISE AND SUTER SIGNINGS YIELD FEW PLAYOFF VICTORIES

 July 4, 2012   HEARTBREAK RATING:

> WHAT HAPPENED:

After the 2011–2012 NHL season, Minnesota Wild owner Craig Leipold began negotiating with free agent defenseman Ryan Suter to play for the Wild. During those negotiations, Suter talked forward Zach Parise into coming to Minnesota too. On July 4, both players signed identical 13-year, $98 million contracts to play for Minnesota. Just like that, we had landed the NHL's top two free agents.

In the seasons that followed, the Wild never won our own division (but did finish second twice). We made the playoffs six times; we lost in the first round four times and in the second round twice. In that time period, the team went through three general managers and three coaches.

> WHY IT HURT SO MUCH:

The entire state of Minnesota seemed to be in love with these signings. Nobody expected the Wild to sign the top free agent—let alone both of them. Plus, Parise was one of us, the son of a North Stars legend and a Minnesotan who came home to play for the hometown team. Unfortunately, the contracts

strapped the team a bit financially. Not only were the contracts guaranteed, they also had "recapture" penalties. This meant that, even if Parise or Suter retired, the team was still required to pay them, and the money would still count against the salary cap, which limited the amount of money a team could spend on its players.

> THE AFTERMATH:

In 2019, the Wild missed the playoffs for the first time since the signings. The team probably needed to rebuild, but it wasn't easy to sit veterans with big contracts in order for younger players to get minutes on the ice. The team was stuck in a sort of purgatory until those contracts expired.

Contracts that last so long are not allowed in the NHL anymore. In 2013, the league adopted a policy that limits a player's contract to eight years with his current team or seven years with a different team.

> DAN'S NOTES:

When a team signs players of that caliber and for that much money, expectations are high. I think most of us believed we would compete for the Stanley Cup. Nevertheless, Minnesota teams have been criticized for not spending money or taking risks. Even though the Parise and Suter contracts have not worked out the way we had hoped, at least Leipold made a bold move that he thought would bring us a championship. The owner deserves credit for being willing to go "all in."

CHAPTER 3
COURT JESTERS

My middle school students missed out on professional basketball in the 1980s. The NBA during that time was loaded with talent. We got to see Larry Bird, Magic Johnson, Michael Jordan, Karl Malone, Isaiah Thomas, and so forth on a nightly basis. When the Minnesota Timberwolves were named an expansion franchise, I was excited. I attended the first game at the Metrodome against the Chicago Bulls. (I still have the "Inaugural Season" poster they gave away that night.) I remember the flashbulbs going off every time Michael Jordan left his feet. My initial excitement for the Timberwolves has faded. Don't get me wrong; I still watch—but it's not easy being a Timberwolves fan. We've had more than our share of bad breaks, beginning with the Minneapolis Lakers and continuing to this day. Read on; you'll see what I mean.

THE MINNEAPOLIS LAKERS' TEAM AIRPLANE GOES MISSING

 January 17, 1960   HEARTBREAK RATING:

> WHAT HAPPENED:

On January 18, 1960, Minneapolis Lakers owner Bob Short was awakened at 2 a.m. by a phone call. It was the Federal Aviation Administration, and they told him that his team's airplane was missing. The plane had taken off in a snowstorm at 8:30 p.m. It was carrying players and family members and was headed back to Minneapolis after the team had lost a game to the Saint Louis Hawks. The twin-engine, propeller-driven, World-War-II-era DC-3 lost electrical power shortly after takeoff. The loss of power prevented the pilots from navigating properly or radioing for help. Guided by the North Star, the pilots pointed the plane in the direction they thought was Minneapolis but flew off course. The pilots had about six hours of fuel in the tanks. After five-and-a-half hours passed, they started flying low and buzzing different towns, looking for a place to land. Residents heard the buzzing and turned on lights to help the plane land safely.

Thirty minutes after the first phone call, Short received another call and learned that his plane had landed in a cornfield in Carroll, Iowa. The passengers were shaken, but miraculously nobody was hurt. Lakers forward Elgin Baylor said that he didn't even realize the plane had touched down and that the landing "was the smoothest thing you ever felt." Strangely enough, the first person to approach the plane on the ground was the town mortician, whose home was one that the plane had buzzed.

> THE AFTERMATH:

On the next trip, the Lakers were scheduled to fly again on the same plane, which the pilots had managed to get back to Minneapolis. Players were understandably nervous about riding in that plane, but they got on board after Short told them they would lose their jobs if they didn't. On the return trip home, players could see fire trucks on the runway as the plane landed. They didn't know that the fire trucks were waiting because one of the plane's engines was on fire.

After the Lakers moved to Los Angeles (page 80), they had one more run-in with that same plane. The team chartered a flight in Chicago. When players arrived, they thought the aircraft looked familiar. According to Steven Aldridge of ESPN, Baylor said, "When we met the owner at the airport, I asked him where he got the plane. He said 'I bought it from some S.O.B. named Bob Short.'"

> SIDE NOTE:

For the 50th anniversary of the infamous event, the Los Angeles Lakers donated $25,000 to the city of Carroll, Iowa, to construct a basketball court near the site of the landing. It was dedicated in September 2010 and named Laker Court.

THE MINNEAPOLIS LAKERS MOVE TO LOS ANGELES

 April 27, 1960

HEARTBREAK RATING:

> WHAT HAPPENED:

In the late 1940s and early 1950s the Minneapolis Lakers won five championships. By 1957, with attendance on the decline, owner Ben Berger was looking to sell the team. That spring, a group of investors purchased the Lakers and kept the team in Minneapolis. But the Lakers didn't have a permanent home; they bounced between three arenas in Minneapolis and Saint Paul. Faced with similar attendance problems and dwindling finances, the owners started scheduling a few "home" games in other cities, including Los Angeles (L.A.), to gauge interest in the team. On April 26, 1960, the Coliseum Commission in L.A. gave approval for the Lakers to lease the facility if the NBA would allow the Lakers to move. The following day, the NBA directors approved the Lakers' move to L.A.

> WHY IT HURT SO MUCH:

The Lakers were a dynasty before sports dynasties were a thing. They won six championships in a seven-year period. The fact that our fans didn't attend enough games to keep them here is sad, especially considering how the Timberwolves have fared, making the playoffs just nine times in the team's first 30 years and losing in the first round every time but one (page 91).

THE AFTERMATH:

Professional basketball returned to Minnesota in 1967 when the American Basketball Association (ABA) was formed. The league, headquartered in Minneapolis, named former Minneapolis Laker George Mikan as its commissioner. Minnesota was awarded one of the league's first franchises: the Muskies. Coached by former Minneapolis Laker Jim Pollard, the Muskies finished the regular season with a 50–28 record but lost in the second round of the playoffs. Due to low attendance and financial difficulties, the Muskies moved to Miami after that season and became the Floridians. On June 28, 1968, the ABA's Pittsburgh Pipers moved to Minnesota. The Minnesota Pipers finished the 1968–1969 season with a 36–42 record and lost in the first round of the playoffs. On July 21, 1969, the Pipers moved back to Pittsburgh. Minnesota was without a professional basketball franchise until the Timberwolves arrived in 1989.

Since moving to L.A., the Lakers have won 11 NBA titles and have been led by countless hall-of-famers, such as Kareem Abdul-Jabbar, Kobe Bryant, Wilt Chamberlain, Magic Johnson, Shaquille O'Neal, Jerry West, and James Worthy. Six Minneapolis Lakers were inducted into the Basketball Hall of Fame: George Mikan (1959), Elgin Baylor (1977), Jim Pollard (1978), Slater Martin (1982), Clyde Lovellette (1988), and Vern Mikkelsen (1995).

SIDE NOTE:

Famed Minnesota Vikings coach Bud Grant played for the Lakers from 1948 to 1951. He averaged 2.6 points per game.

1950 -- WORLD CHA

Left to Right: Slater Martin, Billy Hassett, Don Carlson, Herm Schaefer, Bob

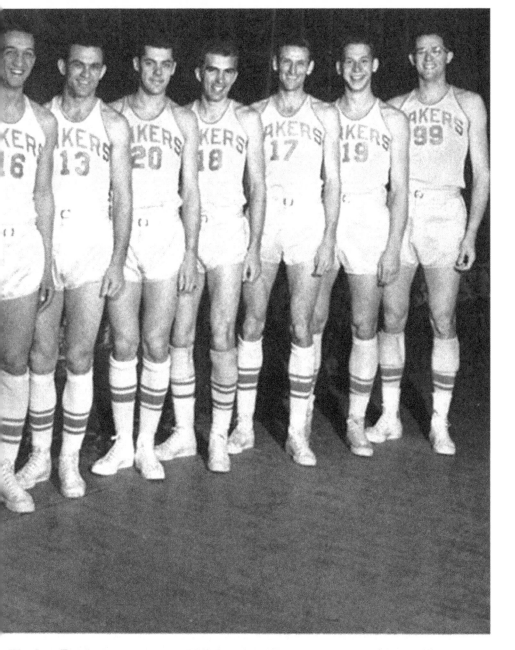

PION LAKERS -- 1950

ASKETBALL ASSOCIATION

, Tony Jaros, Bud Grant, Arnie Ferrin, Jim Pollard, Vern Mikkelsen, George Mikan.

MINNESOTA TRADES AWAY THE FIRST TIMBERWOLF

 October 27, 1989   HEARTBREAK RATING:

> WHAT HAPPENED:

During the 1980s, the NBA's popularity grew exponentially. On April 22, 1987, the NBA voted to expand, creating four new teams. The Charlotte Hornets and the Miami Heat began play in 1988. The Orlando Magic and the Minnesota Timberwolves started in 1989. On June 15, 1989, an expansion draft was held for the Magic and Timberwolves, in which they could choose unprotected players from other teams. With the second pick in that draft, the Timberwolves selected the infamous "Bad Boy" Rick Mahorn (known for his physical style of play) from the Detroit Pistons. Local media was ecstatic about Mahorn being selected and declared the pick the team's first victory.

The Pistons had won the NBA championship two days earlier. On the day the Pistons held their victory parade, Mahorn was told about being selected by the Timberwolves. He was officially on our roster for three months and did some promotional events, but he never reported to training camp. He demanded that his contract be renegotiated or that he be traded. He threatened to retire and even signed a contract to play in Italy. (The Timberwolves threated legal action if he did.) On October 27, after a month of drama, Minnesota traded

Mahorn to the Philadelphia 76ers for a first-round draft pick in 1990 and second-round picks in 1991 and 1992.

> WHY IT HURT SO MUCH:

If selecting Mahorn was our first victory, then trading him was our first defeat. The Timberwolves seemed cursed with bad luck after that.

> THE AFTERMATH:

Our Wolves got their first win on November 10, 1989, against Mahorn and the 76ers. He played two seasons in Philadelphia, along with hall-of-famer Charles Barkley. Together, they were known as "Thump and Bump." Mahorn also played with the New Jersey Nets before returning to Detroit in 1996. After retiring from the NBA, he coached for the WNBA's Detroit Shock with former "Bad Boy" teammate Bill Laimbeer. He later became a color commentator for Pistons radio broadcasts.

> DAN'S NOTES:

On September 9, 1989, Mahorn participated in a promotional event called Hoopfest in downtown Minneapolis. There was a three-on-three tournament in which three lucky KSTP viewers got to play against the first three Timberwolves: Rick Mahorn, Tyrone Corbin, and Pooh Richardson. I was one of those lucky viewers. That Saturday morning, I put on the only NBA shirt I had: a Michael Jordan T-shirt. Mahorn approached me and playfully started shoving me for the cameras. In doing so, he ripped the shirt. I feel terrible that I welcomed the first Timberwolf to Minnesota with a shirt of his hated rival.

TIMBERWOLVES OWNERS TRY TO SELL TO NEW ORLEANS

 May 23, 1994   HEARTBREAK RATING: ♥♥♥♥♥

> WHAT HAPPENED:

When Target Center was built in the late 1980s, the Minnesota Timberwolves' owners, Marv Wolfenson and Harvey Ratner, claimed it would remain privately owned, unlike the other sports facilities in town. However, their financing for the facility buried them in debt. They hoped to have other tenants, most notably a hockey team (page 67), to share the facility and lease space from them, but that never happened. In 1993, the owners threatened to move the Wolves if the city of Minneapolis didn't buy the facility to help them pay off their mortgage. Negotiations took place with Governor Arne Carlson and the Minnesota Legislature, and they approved a deal to purchase the facility and make it publicly owned. After all of that political wrangling, Wolfenson and Ratner tried to sell the team to New Orleans on May 23, 1994.

> WHY IT HURT SO MUCH:

Minnesotans were still grieving the loss of our Minnesota North Stars a year earlier (page 36). The thought of losing another franchise made us numb. It certainly added to our mistrust of sports teams' owners.

Christian Laettner
averaged 16.3 points
per game in 1994–1995.

> THE AFTERMATH:

The deal needed to be approved by the league. On June 15, 1994, commissioner David Stern and the NBA blocked the sale, forcing the team to play the upcoming season in Minneapolis. Glen Taylor swooped in and, after only a week of negotiations, agreed to buy the Timberwolves on August 5. For all the grief that Taylor has received for making decisions that hurt the franchise, we often forget that he saved our Timberwolves and deserves credit for that.

MINNESOTA CAUGHT MAKING SECRET DEAL WITH JOE SMITH

 September 8, 2000   HEARTBREAK RATING:

> WHAT HAPPENED:

Center Joe Smith was a former number-one overall pick, selected by the Golden State Warriors in 1995. In January 1999, he became a free agent after a financial dispute between players and owners led to a lockout. After the lockout, Smith was a hotly sought-after free agent. On January 22, 1999, the Minnesota Timberwolves and Smith agreed to a one-year deal worth $1.75 million. Most believed that was well below Smith's value. As it turned out, the Wolves and Smith had agreed to a secret plan that violated league rules: The contract was going to be the first of three (one-year) deals, which would allow the Timberwolves to obtain Smith's "Bird rights"—a salary-cap exception that let a team exceed the salary cap to re-sign their own players. Once the Wolves obtained Smith's Bird rights, the team could spend over the cap and "reward" him with a large contract. The secret was revealed when Smith's agents, Andy Miller and Eric Fleisher, parted ways.

On September 8, 2000, Timberwolves owner Glen Taylor was called to NBA commissioner David Stern's office to answer questions about the deal. Taylor admitted to everything. Kevin McHale, Minnesota's vice president of basketball operations,

Joe Smith averaged 10.3 points per game in his four seasons with Minnesota.

said that he never looked closely at contracts. McHale also said that teams made those kinds of deals often, adding, "They're just good at it. We're bad." The Timberwolves were fined $3.5 million and lost our first-round picks for five years.

> WHY IT HURT SO MUCH:

The Wolves made the playoffs most of those years, so we wouldn't have had high draft picks. But there was talent available later in the drafts. Losing that many first-round picks made it tougher to build for the future, and it put more pressure on the team to sign free agents.

> THE AFTERMATH:

Smith's contract was voided, and he signed with Detroit for a year. He eventually came back to Minnesota, but the damage was done. On December 8, 2000, McHale and Taylor agreed to a settlement with the NBA. McHale took an unpaid leave of absence until July 31, 2001. Taylor was suspended until August 31, 2001. In return, the Timberwolves got back our 2003 draft pick. (We used it on Ndudi Ebi, who played in a total of 19 games over two seasons.) In December 2001, NBA commissioner David Stern reinstated the Timberwolves' 2005 draft pick. Thanks to our luck with the NBA lottery (page 14), the Wolves got the 14th pick—out of 14 lottery teams. Minnesota used that pick on Rashad McCants. He lasted four years in the league. After the 2003–2004 season, the Timberwolves did not make the playoffs again until 2018. Surprising to many Wolves' fans, McHale was named the best general manager in all sports in 2007 by *Forbes Magazine*.

SAM CASSELL'S DANCE INJURY COSTS A TRIP TO NBA FINALS

 May 8, 2004   HEARTBREAK RATING:

> WHAT HAPPENED:

The Minnesota Timberwolves had made the playoffs seven years in a row but had lost in the first round each year. In the 2003–2004 season, the Wolves finished first in our conference with a 58–24 record, the best in franchise history. It was the second-best record in the NBA that year, behind the Indiana Pacers (61–21). The team was led by Sam Cassell, Kevin Garnett, and Latrell Sprewell. After beating the Denver Nuggets in the first round, Minnesota advanced to the Western Conference Semifinals against the Sacramento Kings. Cassell hit a key shot with 24 seconds left in Game 2 of the series. After doing so, he did a mildly obscene celebration referred to as the "Big Balls Dance." It was meant to visually declare that Cassell was clutch enough to make a big shot when the team needed it. (The Timberwolves won the game, 94–89.)

The Timberwolves beat the Kings in seven games and advanced to the Western Conference Finals against the Los Angeles Lakers. Cassell's play was limited due to a hip injury called an "avulsion fracture." Timberwolves coach Flip Saunders believed the injury had been caused by Cassell performing his dance. The series lasted six games, and Cassell essentially

missed four of them. The Wolves split those games and lost the series, four games to two.

> WHY IT HURT SO MUCH:

If Cassell had been healthy, Minnesota was good enough to advance to the NBA Finals and possibly win a championship.

> THE AFTERMATH:

On October 31, 2004, the night before the next season started, Minnesota offered a reported three-year, $27 million extension to Sprewell. He felt the offer was insulting and turned it down. He was quoted as saying, "Why would I want to help them win a title? They're not doing anything for me. I've got a lot at risk here. I've got my family to feed." Saunders was fired mid-season and was replaced by Kevin McHale. The Timberwolves finished ninth in the Western Conference and missed the playoffs. (In fact, the Timberwolves went 14 years between playoff games.) After the 2004–2005 season, Sprewell did not play in the NBA again. Cassell joined the Los Angeles Clippers for a few seasons and finished his career with the Boston Celtics in 2008. Saunders returned to the Timberwolves in 2013 as president of basketball operations and coached the team in 2014. Tragically, he lost his battle with cancer in 2015.

> DAN'S NOTES:

Some reports claim that Cassell's dance occurred in Game 7 of the series. With the help of KFAN Radio's Scott Korzenowski, we proved through photographic evidence that the infamous dance was indeed performed in Game 2.

KEVIN GARNETT GETS TRADED TO THE BOSTON CELTICS

 July 31, 2007   HEARTBREAK RATING:

> WHAT HAPPENED:

The Minnesota Timberwolves finished the 2006–2007 season 13th out of 15 teams in the Western Conference, yet we had one of the highest payrolls in the NBA. All-star Kevin Garnett wanted to win a championship, and owner Glen Taylor thought it was time to rebuild. After 12 seasons in a Wolves uniform— and just three years after a deep playoff run (page 91)— Minnesota traded Garnett to the Boston Celtics for five players and two first-round draft picks. It was the largest number of players traded for a single player in NBA history. On the day Garnett was introduced to the Boston media, he commented about his former organization no longer being loyal to him, and he gave the impression that he didn't feel appreciated in Minnesota.

> WHY IT HURT SO MUCH:

Garnett was one of the team's few draft successes. He was a team leader, the fans' favorite Timberwolf, and the best player in franchise history. At the time of his trade, Minnesota had only been to the playoffs eight times, and Garnett had played on each of those teams. He set team records for total points, assists, rebounds, and a number of other categories. Many

Kevin Garnett is the greatest player in Wolves history.

Minnesota basketball fans grew up with Garnett as their hero. To see him traded away really stung.

> THE AFTERMATH:

The following season, Garnett and the Celtics won the NBA championship. The players whom the Wolves received in the trade didn't last. Al Jefferson and Ryan Gomes stayed for three years. After six seasons in Boston, Garnett signed with the Brooklyn Nets. He was there for a season and a half, and the team got as far as the Eastern Conference Semifinals in 2014.

On February 19, 2015, Garnett was traded back to the Wolves for Thaddeus Young. Garnett played in 43 games with Minnesota during the final season and a half of his career. He retired in 2016. On February 13, 2020, the Celtics announced that they would retire Garnett's number during the 2020–2021 season. This was frustrating for our fans because Garnett's number was not retired by the Timberwolves.

> DAN'S NOTES:

Garnett won the championship in Boston alongside Ray Allen, a hall-of-famer who was drafted by Minnesota in 1996. We traded him on draft night for Stephon Marbury. After Garnett retired, reports surfaced that he wanted to buy the Timberwolves but did not wish to be a part of any ownership group that included owner Glen Taylor. (Garnett's feud with Taylor reportedly began in 2015 and stemmed from Garnett not getting a front-office job that he believed he was promised.)

TIMBERWOLVES CHOOSE NOT TO DRAFT STEPH CURRY, TWICE

 June 25, 2009   HEARTBREAK RATING: 💔💔💔💔💔

> WHAT HAPPENED:

A month ahead of the NBA draft in 2009, the Minnesota Timberwolves hired David Kahn as the president of basketball operations. The team had two top-10 picks to work with. Kahn selected point guard Ricky Rubio from Spain with the fifth pick in the draft. With pick number six, he chose another point guard: Jonny Flynn out of Syracuse. The next pick belonged to the Golden State Warriors; they took point guard Steph Curry.

> WHY IT HURT SO MUCH:

Curry was a hot commodity heading into the draft. He had become a household name after leading his underdog Davidson Wildcats (a 10th seed) to the Elite Eight in the 2008 NCAA Division I Men's Basketball Tournament. Not only did we pass on him, we passed on him *twice!* Curry became one of the best players in the NBA.

> THE AFTERMATH:

Rubio wouldn't join the Timberwolves until two years later due to buyout clauses with his team in Spain. Even though he was a fan favorite, he missed time due to injury. He was often criticized for his relatively poor shooting abilities. He played

Stephen Curry won three NBA championships.

in Minnesota for six seasons before being traded to the Utah Jazz. Flynn lasted a total of three seasons in the NBA. Curry led the Warriors to three NBA championships and won the NBA's award for MVP twice. Kahn's contract was not renewed with the Timberwolves; he left the team in May 2013.

> DAN'S NOTES:

With the draft's 18th pick, we selected another point guard. Wolves star Kevin Love reacted on Twitter by posting, "What are we doing?????" We traded the pick later that night.

JIMMY BUTLER REQUESTS TO BE TRADED OUT OF MINNESOTA

 September 19, 2018   HEARTBREAK RATING:

> WHAT HAPPENED:

In the summer of 2017, the Minnesota Timberwolves traded for all-star Jimmy Butler of the Chicago Bulls. Butler was a six-year veteran who had averaged 23.9 points per game the previous season. Butler's presence was immediately felt, and our team made the playoffs for the first time in 14 years.

Expectations were high ahead of the next season. However, Butler had reportedly grown frustrated with star teammates Karl-Anthony Towns and Andrew Wiggins. The week before training camp was set to begin, Wolves officials met with Butler, and he demanded to be traded. Initially, he did not report to training camp. He finally showed up to the Timberwolves' facility on October 10, 2018, and played in a scrimmage alongside the team's reserves. Apparently, Butler and company defeated the other starters. Butler screamed and swore at owner Glen Taylor and other front office personnel: "You [expletive] need me!" and "You can't win without me!"

Former Timberwolves' legend Kevin Garnett was asked to comment on the situation when interviewed on TNT's *NBA Tip-Off*. Garnett defended Butler saying, ". . . he's dealing with

Glen [Taylor], who doesn't know [expletive] about basketball." Butler missed three of the first 13 games that season due to "general soreness" before being traded to the Philadelphia 76ers on November 10.

> WHY IT HURT SO MUCH:

It's been nearly impossible for the Timberwolves to attract star players in free agency—or via trade, for that matter. So Butler's arrival was exciting for Minnesota sports fans. He was among the league's best players, and there were rumors ahead of the 2017 trade that he actually wanted to come here. When he did arrive, it appeared that Butler, Towns, and Wiggins would finally form the "big three" that our team needed to compete in the NBA. The sudden and unexpected turn of events that led to his departure pulled the rug out from under us.

> THE AFTERMATH:

Butler's 76ers made the playoffs at the end of the 2018–2019 regular season. They beat the Brooklyn Nets in the first round but lost to the Toronto Raptors in the second round. The Timberwolves finished with a disappointing record of 36–46, which was 11 fewer wins than the season before.

> DAN'S NOTES:

I often listen to sports talk on the radio in my car. One day, during the tail end of this saga, my six-year-old son was with me in the car. He asked, "Daddy, is Jimmy Butler naughty?"

QUICK HITS: TECHNICAL FOULS

> THE TRIALS AND TRIBULATIONS OF J.R. RIDER:

On June 30, 1993, the Minnesota Timberwolves drafted Isaiah "J.R." Rider from the University of Nevada, Las Vegas. Rider was very talented, but drama seemed to follow him. In addition to troubles with the law, he missed team flights and missed practices for reasons such as staying up too late to film a shoe commercial and water pipes bursting inside his house, which, according to media members, was a reason he used more than once. In a 1994 loss to Phoenix, Rider played poorly, sulked to the bench, and sat on the floor by himself. After the game, Timberwolves coach Bill Blair said that Rider needed to grow up. Rider heard about the comment and stormed into the media room. He declared that he was going to have his own press conference. Two days later, he did, talking about his frustrations with his own play (for which he apologized), the coach, and more. In a game against the Utah Jazz in 1996, Rider was ejected. He had to be restrained by teammates, and he wouldn't leave the court until his mother came to calm him down. He tried to return to the court after the first half, but team vice president Kevin McHale got him back into the locker room. On July 23, 1996, Rider was traded to Portland.

> KAHN AND KEVIN:

In 2011, Kevin Love was the best player on the Timberwolves. He wanted to get a five-year contract extension, but the team offered a four-year deal instead. Negotiations got heated; at one point, general manager David Kahn reportedly shoved a contract into Love's hands. Love eventually signed the four-year deal, but he continued to criticize management about the direction of the team. Sensing that Love would opt out of his contract after the upcoming season, the Wolves traded Love to Cleveland on August 23, 2014. Just like Garnett (page 93), Love won an NBA championship with his new team.

Dan's Notes: It seemed clear that Love was going to leave. I remember being ecstatic that we got *anything* for him. Getting the player who had been the first-overall draft pick . . . that was even better. Right? Be careful what you wish for.

> GAZING INTO ANDREW WIGGINS' EYES:

As part of the Kevin Love trade in 2014, the Wolves acquired Andrew Wiggins, who'd been drafted first overall by Cleveland that summer. In his first season, Wiggins won the NBA Rookie of the Year Award. Yet by his fourth season (the final year of his contract), Wiggins had underachieved by most accounts. Perhaps it was an overreaction to what had gone down with Love, but the Wolves wanted to give Wiggins a maximum deal, typically reserved for the top players in the league. Before he would do so, team owner Glen Taylor wanted to make sure that Wiggins was committed to improving and wanted to "look [him] in the eye." On October 11, 2017, Wiggins signed a five-year, $147 million deal. He didn't play as well as other "max deal" stars around the league. On February 6, 2020, the Wolves traded him and the team's first- and second-round draft picks in 2021 to the Golden State Warriors for D'Angelo Russell.

CHAPTER 4
DIAMOND IN THE ROUGH

I n the early 1900s, Clark Griffith was manager of the Washington Senators. After managing the team for eight years, he grew frustrated with the team owners and their lack of spending on players' salaries. On December 13, 1919, he bought a controlling interest in the team. He came to have a penny-pinching reputation of his own in terms of how he ran his business, stadium, and players' salaries. Clark passed his frugal philosophy on to his nephew and adopted son, Calvin Griffith. When Clark died in 1955, Calvin took over the team, which he moved to Minnesota in 1961. The team was renamed the Twins, for the Twin Cities. Calvin, too, gained a reputation for being frugal. He sold the Twins to Carl Pohlad in 1984, but the franchise's spending philosophy didn't seem to change very much—as some of the entries in this chapter suggest. Over the years, many fans and media members have expressed frustration over the team's relative lack of spending.

THE MINNESOTA TWINS LOSE THE 1965 WORLD SERIES

 October 14, 1965   HEARTBREAK RATING: ♥♥♥♥♥

WHAT HAPPENED:

Led by players like Harmon Killebrew, Tony Oliva, Earl Battey, Jim "Mudcat" Grant, and Jim Kaat, the Minnesota Twins won 102 games in 1965, the most wins in a season in team history. Our club finished first in the AL, seven games ahead of the Chicago White Sox. As winners of the AL, the Twins faced the Los Angeles Dodgers, champions of the NL, in the World Series. Zoilo Versalles powered the Twins in Game 1, with four RBIs. Grant pitched a gem of a game, and Minnesota won, 8–2. In Game 2, Kaat was the winning pitcher, leading the Twins to victory, 5–1.

After two wins at Metropolitan Stadium in Bloomington, the Twins traveled to Dodger Stadium in Los Angeles for Games 3, 4, and 5. Minnesota managed just two runs in 27 innings against pitchers Claude Osteen, Don Drysdale, and Sandy Koufax. The Twins lost all three games.

The World Series returned to Minnesota for the final two games. The Twins bounced back in Game 6. Grant held the Dodgers to one run and hit a home run in the Twins' 5–1 win. Game 7, however, was dominated by the Dodgers' Koufax. He threw

Harmon Killebrew was with the Washington Senators when they moved to Minnesota.

a three-hit shutout to clinch the Series for Los Angeles—but he got a bit of help from his third-baseman, Junior Gilliam. Down 2–0 in the fifth inning, the Twins had runners on first and second base. Versalles hit a ball that would likely have been a double that tied the game. However, Gilliam made a miraculous stop and threw Versalles out at first base. After the next batter grounded out, the inning ended—and so did the Twins' chances.

> WHY IT HURT SO MUCH:

This was the Twins' first appearance in the World Series. We had home-field advantage and were up, two games to none. We even beat Koufax in Game 2. In Games 5 and 7, however, Koufax threw 18 shutout innings. Twins manager Sam Mele said, "It took the best pitcher in baseball to finally kill us off."

> THE AFTERMATH:

The Twins did not return to the World Series until 1987. The Dodgers got back to the World Series in 1966, 1974, 1977, and 1978; their next championship came in 1981.

> DAN'S NOTES:

Not only did Metropolitan Stadium play host to the World Series in 1965, but it also hosted the MLB All-Star Game that summer. The AL roster was loaded with Twins. Battey, Grant, Jimmie Hall, Killebrew, Oliva, and Versalles were all on the team. Killebrew hit a home run in the game.

MINNESOTA TWINS GET SWEPT IN AL CHAMPIONSHIP

 October 6, 1969   HEARTBREAK RATING: ♥♥♥♥♡

> WHAT HAPPENED:

The 1969 season was the first time MLB separated the AL and NL into Eastern and Western divisions, so it was also the first season with championship series. The Minnesota Twins finished first in the AL West with a record of 97–65 and advanced to play the Baltimore Orioles in the AL Championship Series (ALCS). The Orioles had a whopping 109–53 record. In Game 1, the Twins led, 3–2, in the bottom of the ninth inning. The Orioles tied the score with a home run and then won in the 12th inning on a squeeze bunt. Game 2 also went into extra innings. This time, the Orioles won, 1–0, on an RBI single in the 11th inning. Game 3 was played in Minnesota, and the home team was blown out, 11–2, giving Baltimore a series sweep.

> WHY IT HURT SO MUCH:

This was the Twins' first postseason appearance since the 1965 World Series loss. It's hard to win a best-of-five series after losing the first two games, and we lost by such slim margins. If those first two games had gone the other way, maybe we could've tried our luck against the famed Miracle Mets in the 1969 World Series.

Rod Carew had
a .332 batting
average in 1969.

> THE AFTERMATH:

Owner Calvin Griffith was unhappy with manager Billy Martin about a few events that occurred during the season. When Minnesota Senator Hubert Humphrey wanted to visit the locker room after a loss, Martin refused to let him in. There was also a fight between Martin and pitcher Dave Boswell at one point. Griffith was also reportedly upset that star pitcher Jim Kaat didn't play in Game 3 of the ALCS. (Kaat had been injured during the regular season, and Martin felt that he had not been pitching well.) Martin was not rehired. In his place, the Twins made Bill Rigney the manager.

In 1970, the Twins again won the AL West and again were swept by the Orioles. Unlike the previous season, Kaat pitched in Game 3. He gave up two earned runs and four total runs in two innings. Baltimore clinched the series with a 6–1 win. They went on to win the 1970 World Series versus the Cincinnati Reds, four games to one. Billy Martin won the 1977 World Series as manager of the New York Yankees.

> DAN'S NOTES:

On August 25, 1970, a bomb threat halted a game between the Twins and the Boston Red Sox at Met Stadium. In the fourth inning, fans were told to leave the stadium, but many went onto the field to wait while police searched the premises. The game resumed 43 minutes later. The Twins lost the game, 1–0, on an eighth-inning home run by the Red Sox's Tony Conigliaro off Twins pitcher Tom Hall.

BERT BLYLEVEN GIVES UP TWO INSIDE-THE-PARK HOME RUNS

 July 31, 1972   HEARTBREAK RATING:

> WHAT HAPPENED:

In the middle of the 1972 MLB season, the Chicago White Sox and the Minnesota Twins were both chasing the division-leading Oakland Athletics. The Twins were 8.5 games back, and the White Sox were 5.5 back. Minnesota had a chance to gain some ground on July 31 when we hosted the White Sox. In the top of the first inning, with two runners on base, Chicago's power-hitting first baseman Dick Allen looped a single into center field off Twins pitcher Bert Blyleven. The grass was slippery, thanks to a morning rain shower, and outfielder Bobby Darwin slipped while trying to play the ball. It bounced over him. The two runners scored, and so did Allen, who managed a rare inside-the-park home run.

History repeated itself in the fifth inning. With a runner on second base, Allen hit a ball deep to left center field. Darwin attempted to make a difficult catch but couldn't get to the ball in time. It bounced off the wall and away from Darwin, giving Allen the time he needed to score again—another inside-the-park home run. Blyleven lasted just four and a third innings. He gave up six earned runs. The White Sox won the game, 8–1.

Blyleven helped the Twins win the 1987 World Series.

> THE AFTERMATH:

The Athletics won the division and the World Series. The White Sox finished 5.5 games back, and the Twins were 15.5 games back. Blyleven won 17 games with a 2.73 earned run average. Allen led MLB with 37 home runs and 113 runs batted in. On October 4, 1986, the Twins' Greg Gagne hit two inside-the-park home runs in one game. He did it against White Sox pitcher Floyd Bannister. Minnesota won, 7–3, and the winning pitcher was Bert Blyleven.

ROD CAREW SAYS HE'LL NEVER SIGN WITH THE TWINS AGAIN

 October 1, 1978   HEARTBREAK RATING:

> WHAT HAPPENED:

Minnesota Twins infielder Rod Carew was the AL Rookie of the Year in 1967. In 1977, he won the AL award for MVP. He made $180,000 that year, which was far less than other stars were paid. (The Philadelphia Phillies' Mike Schmidt—the highest paid player in MLB—earned $560,000.) Carew wanted to stay with the Twins, but his salary had to be competitive. Contract negotiations took place in the summer of 1977 and again in March of 1978. Twins owner Calvin Griffith offered Carew a two-year extension worth about $240,000 per year. Carew felt that he was worth more and also wanted a longer deal.

In May, the Twins invited pitcher Mike Marshall to try out for the team. Marshall impressed the coaches, but Griffith didn't sign him. Carew became frustrated; he felt that Marshall would help the team win. A few days later, Carew said that he would never sign with the Twins again. Griffith signed Marshall the next day. Marshall went on to save 21 games for Minnesota that season (and led the league with 32 saves in 1979). On September 28, 1978, Griffith publicly called Carew a "damn fool" and made troubling racist remarks, including a suggestion that he moved the team from Washington, D.C., to Minnesota because fewer

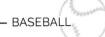

African Americans lived here. On October 1, Carew reaffirmed that he would "never sign another contract" with the Twins.

> WHY IT HURT SO MUCH:

Carew was one of the best players in the league, and, for a time, he wanted to finish his career in Minnesota. Sid Hartman was arguably the most optimistic sports media personality in the state, yet even he was upset. He wrote in *The Minneapolis Tribune*, "Well, Calvin, if Carew goes, you might as well go with him because the last of your fans will disappear."

> THE AFTERMATH:

On December 7, 1978, Griffith traded Carew to the NL's San Francisco Giants. Carew wanted to remain in the AL, so he refused to report, nullifying the deal. Griffith began negotiating with the New York Yankees and California Angels. The Twins and Yankees were close to a deal, but the Yankees withdrew their offer after Griffith asked for more players. The Twins made what Hartman called an "inferior trade" on February 3, 1979. Carew was sent to the Angels for Ken Landreaux, Paul Hartzell, and prospects Dave Engle and Brad Havens. The Angels paid Carew $800,000 in 1979, and by 1984 he was making more than $1 million per year. He retired after the 1985 season.

Carew was an 18-time All-Star, won seven batting titles, and was elected to the National Baseball Hall of Fame in 1991. He said that he put everything with Griffith behind him, and he was seen hanging out in the Twins dugout at Target Field from time to time.

MINNESOTA TWINS FAIL TO SIGN THE #1 OVERALL DRAFT PICK

 June 6, 1983 HEARTBREAK RATING:

> WHAT HAPPENED:

After finishing the 1982 season with 102 losses, the Minnesota Twins earned the number-one overall draft pick for the first time in franchise history. Our team set their sights on pitcher Tim Belcher from Mount Vernon Nazarene University in Ohio. Before the draft, Belcher informed the Twins that he'd be looking for a minimum signing bonus of $125,000. (In comparison, the draft's second pick, Kurt Stillwell, signed for $140,000, so asking for $125,000 wasn't out of the norm.) The Twins had never paid that large of a bonus before. Our club drafted Belcher and offered him a signing bonus of $90,000. Not surprisingly, Belcher declined. Twins owner Calvin Griffith withdrew the offer of $90,000 and submitted a new offer of $60,000. Other owners expressed bewilderment. Some believed that, at worst, Griffith could've signed Belcher and traded him for $200,000. Belcher never signed with the Twins.

After losing the pitcher, Griffith said, "It won't be the first time we've lost something." When he was challenged about it being the only first overall pick in team history, Griffith replied, "And I hope we never have it again."

WHY IT HURT SO MUCH:

The Twins finally had the top pick, and we managed to screw it up—over money. Belcher would have been a nice addition to our teams of the late 1980s—and maybe we could have won a few more championships. We'll never know.

THE AFTERMATH:

On January 17, 1984, Belcher became the first overall selection of MLB's secondary phase draft. He was chosen by the New York Yankees (and signed for $125,000). He ended up in the Oakland Athletics' minor-league system and was eventually traded to the Los Angeles Dodgers. He pitched in the league for 14 seasons and won 10 or more games in nine seasons. He helped the Dodgers win the World Series in 1988. His best year was 1989, when he went 15–12 with a 2.82 earned run average (ERA) and 200 strikeouts.

DAN'S NOTES:

The Twins' second-round pick in the 1983 draft was another pitcher, Bill Swift. Minnesota offered him a $45,000 signing bonus. Swift turned down the offer and went back to school. He was drafted the following year by the Seattle Mariners. He joined the San Francisco Giants in 1992 and was 10–4 with a 2.08 ERA, the lowest in the league. In 1993, his record was 21–8, and he posted a 2.82 ERA. He finished second in voting for the NL's Cy Young Award, given to the best pitcher.

TWINS PITCHER JOE NIEKRO IS EJECTED FOR CHEATING

 August 3, 1987   HEARTBREAK RATING:

> WHAT HAPPENED:

Joe Niekro was a knuckleball pitcher who played with several teams over his 22-year career. He came to Minnesota in a trade with the New York Yankees on June 7, 1987. Two months later, the Twins were playing the California Angels in Anaheim. In the fourth inning, Niekro threw a pitch that home plate umpire (and Saint Paul, Minnesota, native) Tim Tschida felt moved a little too much. Tschida approached the mound and asked Niekro to give him the ball and his glove. After surrendering the ball, Niekro dramatically flipped his glove to Tschida. Niekro then started to put his hands in his back pockets but was stopped by second base umpire Steve Palermo, who asked Niekro to empty his pockets. Niekro attempted to flip out his pockets and raise his arms in innocence. As he did so, he threw an emery board with his right hand and tried to put sandpaper into catcher Sal Butera's glove with his left. The umpires weren't fooled. They immediately ejected Niekro from the game. The Twins won, 11–3.

> THE AFTERMATH:

Niekro claimed that the emery board was for his fingernails that got roughed up, which was normal for a knuckleball pitcher.

Joe Niekro
tossed his glove to
the umpire for inspection.

He added that the sandpaper was for filing down blisters. Two days after the incident, Niekro was suspended for 10 games. He took advantage of his sudden notoriety and made a guest appearance on *Late Night with David Letterman*, at which he walked onto the stage wearing a tool belt with an attached power sander. When Letterman asked if he had doctored the baseballs, Niekro's response was "Do I look like a doctor?" The Twins won the World Series that year. Niekro made just one appearance: He pitched two scoreless innings in Game 4.

PITCHER JACK MORRIS LEAVES TWINS TO SIGN WITH TORONTO

 December 18, 1991   HEARTBREAK RATING: 💔💔💔💔💔

WHAT HAPPENED:

A native of Saint Paul, Minnesota, Jack Morris was drafted by the Detroit Tigers in 1976. He pitched with Detroit for 14 seasons and led them to the World Series in 1984. In 1991, the Tigers offered Morris $9.3 million to stay, but Morris instead signed a one-year, $3.5 million deal to come home and play with the Minnesota Twins.

Morris won 18 games that season and another four games in the postseason—including two wins in the ALCS against the Toronto Blue Jays. The other two postseason wins came in the World Series versus the Atlanta Braves. In the deciding Game 7, Morris pitched a 10-inning masterpiece, during which he gave up seven hits and no runs. He out-dueled Braves' ace John Smoltz and won the game, 1–0. His performance helped the Twins clinch our second championship in five seasons. Morris was named the World Series MVP.

Because of that success, Morris was going to command more money on the free-agent market. He had lunch with team owner Carl Pohlad to discuss the possibility of staying with the team. According to Morris, Pohlad advised him to take a deal with another team because the Twins were saving money to re-sign all-star outfielder Kirby Puckett. On December 18, Morris signed a guaranteed two-year deal with the Blue Jays, which paid the pitcher $10.85 million per year.

> WHY IT HURT SO MUCH:

Morris was a hometown hero, and he wanted to stay. It was a major disappointment that the team didn't bring him back after such a successful season. Plus, many baseball experts believed that the Twins had a good shot at repeating as champions in 1992. Without Morris, the team was a respectable 90–72, but we finished six games behind the Oakland Athletics and missed the playoffs.

> THE AFTERMATH:

Morris and the Blue Jays won the World Series in 1992 and again in 1993. The pitcher played for the Cleveland Indians in 1994 and for the minor league Saint Paul Saints in 1996. He was elected to the National Baseball Hall of Fame in 2018.

> DAN'S NOTES:

Morris recounted his infamous lunch with Pohlad on KFAN Radio's *Dan Barreiro Show*. After Morris said that Pohlad was saving money for Puckett, Barreiro replied, "Did you tell Carl that it wasn't illegal to save [his money] for two guys?"

TWINS OWNER SIGNS LETTER OF INTENT TO MOVE THE TEAM

 October 3, 1997   HEARTBREAK RATING: ♥♥♥♥♥

> WHAT HAPPENED:

In the mid-1990s, Minnesota Twins owner Carl Pohlad toured the newly built Jacobs Field in Cleveland, Ohio. He became enamored with the idea of getting a new outdoor stadium. In September 1995, Twins officials informed a legislative task force that the Metrodome (barely 13 years old) could not generate the revenue needed for the Twins to remain competitive. The Legislature denied public funding for a new stadium, so MLB gave Pohlad permission to sell the team. On September 7, 1997, the *Star Tribune's* Patrick Reusse reported that the Twins had an offer from NationsBank in Charlotte, North Carolina. They were reportedly willing to buy the team outright or build a stadium so Pohlad could move. Later that day, Pohlad denied it, saying, "I wish that were true." Another group from North Carolina, led by businessman Don Beaver, was also interested in the Twins. On October 3, Pohlad signed a letter of intent to sell his team to Beaver, who planned to move the team to North Carolina.

> WHY IT HURT SO MUCH:

The 1990s were hard on Minnesota sports fans. Norm Green moved the North Stars (page 36). Marv Wolfenson and Harvey Ratner tried to move the Timberwolves (page 86). Even the

Vikings' stability fell into question with the 1997 announcement that they were for sale. The Twins took a turn too. The team was potentially leaving, which was almost too much for our sports fans to take.

> THE AFTERMATH:

From the start, there was skepticism about whether voters in North Carolina would approve public funding for a new stadium. On May 5, 1998, North Carolina voters officially rejected a referendum to pay for a stadium. It effectively killed the deal. On July 22, the Twins reached a new lease agreement with the Metrodome. On December 23, Pohlad announced that the team would slash its payroll from $27 million in 1998 to $10–$15 million in 1999. By the end of 2000 and throughout 2001, rumors swirled about the Twins becoming one of two teams contracted by the league (page 20). At the same time, Alabama businessman Donald Watkins was given permission from the league to purchase a team—such as the Minnesota Twins. Needless to say, none of these possibilities came to be. In February 2006, a Hennepin County District Judge granted Pohlad permission to sell or move the team. Three months later, the Minnesota Legislature passed the "Ballpark Bill," paving the way for Target Field to be built. Pohlad never saw his team play in the new stadium. He died on January 5, 2009, at the age of 93. When he bought the Twins in 1984, he paid around $38 million. When he died, the Twins were worth an estimated $350 million. The first game at Target Field was played on April 12, 2010. The Twins defeated the Boston Red Sox, 5–2.

MINNESOTA TWINS RELEASE DAVID "BIG PAPI" ORTIZ

 December 16, 2002   HEARTBREAK RATING:

> WHAT HAPPENED:

On September 13, 1996, the Minnesota Twins acquired a minor league first baseman as the "player to be named later" in a trade with the Seattle Mariners. His name was David Americo Ortiz Arias. After joining the Twins, he started going by David Ortiz. He rose quickly through the minor-league system in 1997, hitting .317 with 31 home runs. He made his MLB debut that September. In 15 games, he managed a .327 batting average with a home run. In 1998, a wrist injury slowed him down; he only played in 86 games. Manager Tom Kelly reportedly didn't like Ortiz's style of play, specifically his questionable defensive skills at first base and his swing-for-the-fences approach to batting. In 1999, Ortiz didn't hit well in spring training, so he was sent back to the minor leagues. He only played in 10 games with the Twins that season, but he hit .315 with 30 home runs in the minors.

During the next three seasons, Ortiz was mostly utilized as a designated hitter. The more he played, the better he seemed to get. In 2001, he hit 18 home runs, even though he only played in 89 games due to another wrist injury. The following year, he hit .272 with 20 home runs and 75 runs batted in, his best year

David Ortiz went on to have an all-star career in Boston.

in Minnesota. The Twins made the postseason, and Ortiz hit .313 in the ALCS loss to the Anaheim Angels. That offseason he was due $1.5 million in salary arbitration. Rather than pay him an increase in salary (about $500,000 more than the previous season), the Twins released him on December 16, 2002. Twins general manager Terry Ryan said the decision was his; the team had Doug Mientkiewicz at first base and a solid prospect in Justin Morneau. Plus, they wanted to open a roster spot for a shortstop named Jose Morban. Ryan later said that it wasn't a financial decision; "it was a very bad baseball decision."

> WHY IT HURT SO MUCH:

When the Twins let Ortiz go, we had a solid team. If we had kept him, our roster—which included stars like Torii Hunter, Jacque Jones, and Johan Santana—might have been good enough to reach another World Series. Ortiz said that he thought the Twins would have won another championship.

> THE AFTERMATH:

Ortiz signed with the Boston Red Sox on January 22, 2003, for $1.25 million. He hit 31 home runs for the Red Sox and helped them reach the playoffs. In 2004, he led the Red Sox to their first World Series title in 86 years. He rose to become one of the most popular and successful players in MLB. He helped Boston win three World Series (2004, 2007, 2013), and he took part in 10 All-Star Games. Ortiz retired after the 2016 season. During that same span of time, the Twins made the postseason five times and never advanced out of the first round (page 130).

TWINS GET STADIUM, THEN LET TWO TOP PLAYERS LEAVE

 February 2, 2008   HEARTBREAK RATING:

> WHAT HAPPENED:

On May 21, 2007, construction officially began on the stadium that would become Target Field. An official groundbreaking celebration was held on August 30. The Minnesota Twins were in the midst of ace pitcher Johan Santana's eighth season with the team. He was a two-time Cy Young Award winner as the best pitcher in the AL. He was making $13 million, with one more year on his contract. The Twins knew that he would command a record-breaking contract. Also on that 2007 team was center fielder Torii Hunter. Hunter had been drafted by the Twins in 1993. He was a two-time All-Star and a seven-time Gold Glove winner for his outstanding defensive play. He was a leader in the locker room and arguably the fans' favorite player. He was in his 11th season, earning $12 million in the final year of his contract. In October 2007, the Twins hired Bill Smith as general manager. He reportedly offered Hunter a three-year, $45 million deal. Hunter wanted a five-year deal, but the Twins apparently wouldn't budge from three years. On November 22, Hunter agreed to a five-year, $90-million contract with the Los Angeles Angels. He said it wasn't about the money; it was about those two extra years. On February 2, 2008, Smith traded Santana to the New York Mets. Santana signed a six-

Torii Hunter hit 214 home runs in his 12 years in Minnesota.

year, $137 million contract. The Twins received four prospects from the Mets in return: Carlos Gomez, Deolis Guerra, Philip Humber, and Kevin Mulvey.

> WHY IT HURT SO MUCH:

Twins officials had said that a new stadium would help them compete on the field. In other words, they could spend more on players' salaries. Losing two of our best players right after the stadium got approved was extremely disappointing. Even though Target Field wouldn't open until 2010, it felt to some fans as if the Twins had gotten what they wanted and then just shrugged their shoulders at us.

> THE AFTERMATH:

It was rumored that the Twins let both Hunter and Santana go because the team was building for 2010, when the stadium opened. Our Twins did increase their payroll, ranking in the top half of the league from 2010 to 2012. But we dropped to 23rd in 2013. Hunter played with the Angels for five years and with the Detroit Tigers after that. He returned to Minnesota for one season in 2015 and then retired. Santana pitched for the Mets for four years and won 46 games. In 2011, Smith was fired by the Twins and was replaced by Terry Ryan.

> DAN'S NOTES:

Fans were already mourning the loss of Timberwolves star Kevin Garnett. He had been traded to the Boston Celtics in July 2007 (page 93). Baseball commissioner Bud Selig attended the Target Field groundbreaking ceremony. He was booed.

MINNESOTA TWINS LOSE THE MOST GAMES IN TEAM HISTORY

 September 30, 2016   HEARTBREAK RATING:

WHAT HAPPENED:

On November 4, 2014, hall-of-famer and Minnesota native Paul Molitor was introduced as the 13th manager in Twins history. The 2015 season was his first at the helm; it was also the rookie year for highly regarded prospects Miguel Sano and Byron Buxton, as well as Eddie Rosario. The Twins improved to 83–79 that season and finished second in the division. This led to high hopes for 2016. Team leaders felt like the Twins had a shot at winning the division. The day before the season started, second baseman Brian Dozier said, "There's always hype, but this year feels different." The team was brimming with confidence.

The Twins lost the first nine games. A month into the season, our record was 8–20. Twins owner Jim Pohlad said Molitor and general manager Terry Ryan had his support. He added that there wasn't much else they could do and put most of the blame on the players. After falling to 33–58 (the second-worst mid-season record in franchise history), the Twins fired Ryan on July 18. The second half of the season played out like the first. On September 30, the Twins fell to the Chicago White Sox, 7–3, and earned their 103rd loss of the season. The 59–103

mark was the worst record in MLB in 2016 and the worst record in Minnesota Twins history.

WHY IT HURT SO MUCH:

It had been a while since Minnesota Twins fans had reason to hope. Young talent and a successful spring training gave us confidence and got us excited for what was to come. It all came crashing down in the first month and never got better. This was rock bottom. Twins fans have endured a lot of bad seasons, but this one was mathematically the worst.

THE AFTERMATH:

On October 3, 2016, the Twins hired Derek Falvey as chief baseball officer. A month later, Thad Levine joined the team as general manager. The duo ran the front office together. In 2017, the Twins unexpectedly won 85 games, finished second in the division, and earned a trip to the postseason (page 130). Molitor was named the AL Manager of the Year. The following season, the Twins were 78–84 and Molitor was fired. Three weeks later, Rocco Baldelli was introduced as the new manager. His Twins won 101 games in 2018 (the second most wins in Twins history) and the Central Division title. Our team also broke the franchise and MLB records for home runs in a season with 307. Because many of the players on the roster were Spanish-speaking, the team was nicknamed the Bomba Squad—with *Bomba* being Spanish for "bomb" (or home run). Many of the team's top players were acquired during the tenures of former general managers Bill Smith and Terry Ryan.

MINNESOTA TWINS SET RECORD FOR PLAYOFF LOSING STREAK

 September 29, 2020   HEARTBREAK RATING:

 WHAT HAPPENED:

Motivated by the threat of contraction (page 20), the 2002 Minnesota Twins qualified for the postseason for the first time since winning the World Series in 1991. We beat the Oakland Athletics in the AL Division Series (ALDS) and advanced to the AL Championship Series but lost to the Anaheim Angels. For the rest of that decade and through the next, the Twins lost every postseason series in which we played. In 2003, the Twins won Game 1 of the ALDS against the New York Yankees, but we were eliminated after dropping the next three games.

In 2004, Twins ace Johan Santana pitched a gem against the Yankees on October 5. He went seven scoreless innings. Jacque Jones homered and Shannon Stewart went two for four from the plate with a run batted in. The Twins won, 2–0, and took Game 1 of the ALDS. It was Minnesota's last playoff victory in a record-breaking stretch that lasted more than 15 years. The Yankees took the next three games and won the series.

The Oakland Athletics knocked the 2006 Twins out of the ALDS in three games. Three years later, Minnesota finished the season tied with the Detroit Tigers and won a tie-breaker game in 12 innings, 6–5. That victory earned Minnesota a trip to the postseason—and a three-game sweep at the hands of the Yankees. The Twins led early in Game 1 of the series, and we probably should've won Game 2: Our star closing pitcher, Joe Nathan, gave up a two-run home run in the bottom of the ninth inning that sent the game into extra innings. In the top of the 11th, another Twins star, Joe Mauer, came through with a ground-rule double—except the left field umpire, Phil Cuzzi, mistakenly called it a foul ball. That very likely cost Minnesota a run (since the next two batters got hits) and possibly the game.

In 2010, the Twins again lost the ALDS, three games to zip. After that, it was seven years before we returned to the postseason, where . . . guess who: the New York Yankees beat us, 8–4, in a one-game wildcard matchup. Two years later, in 2019, Minnesota was swept yet again by New York. Then, in the pandemic-shortened 2020 season, our team was dispatched by the underdog Houston Astros in a best-of-three series. The first game, a 4–1 defeat on September 29, set a North American record for the most consecutive playoff losses by a pro team. A day later, Houston completed the two-game sweep.

> WHY IT HURT SO MUCH:

This record is an embarrassing one. It's bad enough to set such a deflating record, when every year's regular-season promise ends with a dud. What's worse is that 13 of the 18 losses were to the Yankees. If it's not in the players' heads, it's certainly in the heads of the fans. A matchup with the Yankees fills us with hopelessness and dread.

Joe Mauer was named
the AL MVP in 2009.

QUICK HITS: CHIN MUSIC

STEVE GARVEY REFUSES TWINS DRAFT OFFER:

Steve Garvey was a standout high school athlete. He was an all-city quarterback, and he played third base. He hoped to be in baseball and football in college, but he hadn't ruled out diving right into professional baseball. In the 1966 Amateur Draft, the Minnesota Twins selected Garvey in the third round. The next day, he turned down a deal from the Twins and signed a scholarship offer from Michigan State University. According to the satirical opinion of the *Star Tribune's* Patrick Reusse, Garvey chose college over the Twins because "he probably made the difficult decision to turn down [owner Calvin Griffith's] $3,000 (give or take a few bucks) bonus offer." Garvey was a college All-American in 1968. On June 7, 1968, the Los Angeles Dodgers drafted him. Garvey had a legendary 19-year career. He was named the 1974 NL MVP and was a two-time MVP of the NL Championship Series. He played in four World Series with the Dodgers and won a championship in 1981. He won four Gold Gloves for his defensive play. He played in 10 All-Star Games and won two All-Star MVP awards.

▶ KILLEBREW GETS INJURED IN ALL-STAR GAME:

In the bottom of the third inning of the 1968 MLB All-Star Game, the Cincinnati Reds' Curt Flood hit a ground ball to shortstop Jim Fregosi of the California Angels. Fregosi made a low throw to first base. Twins star Harmon Killebrew, who was playing first base, had to stretch to reach it. Killebrew later said, "The clay gave way under my spikes, and I did a split." Even though he caught the ball and recorded the out, the awkward stretch caused the hamstring in Killebrew's right leg to tear. He missed about two months due to the injury.

> BLYLEVEN'S OBSCENITY:

In the spring of 1976, Twins pitcher Bert Blyleven was in a contract dispute with owner Calvin Griffith. Blyleven demanded to be traded. He was outspokenly critical of the situation, which angered many Twins fans. On May 31, in what turned out to be his last game with the Twins (until his return in 1985), Blyleven headed toward the dugout after pitching the top of the ninth. He was greeted by boos from the stands. A group of fans even sang, "Good Night, Bert." According to *The Minneapolis Tribune's* Joe Soucheray, Blyleven responded by offering them "a short-armed salute" (extended middle finger).

Blyleven was traded to the Texas Rangers the next day. A week later, he did it again in a nationally televised game. The pitcher raised his finger at a camera while in the dugout between innings. Television announcer Al Michaels quipped, "I guess Bert's sending a message to Minnesota." Blyleven later claimed that it wasn't meant to be obscene; he was responding to the cameraman's question: "Who's number one?" When he was with Cleveland in 1985, Blyleven flipped off the Baltimore fans. He later became a television broadcaster for Fox Sports North. On a Twins pregame broadcast in 2006, he said the F-word on live TV when he didn't realize the cameras were rolling.

> CALVIN GRIFFITH'S LIQUIDATION:

In 1982, there were rumors that Twins owner Calvin Griffith was looking to sell the team, so he wanted to cut costs. A few days into the season, he traded Roy Smalley (who had a $600,000 salary) to the New York Yankees for pitcher Ron Davis (with a $300,000 salary), two minor leaguers—one of whom was shortstop Greg Gagne—and $400,000 cash. A month later, the Twins were 11–22 and already 10.5 games out of first place. Griffith traded pitcher Doug Corbett and second baseman Rob Wilfong to the California Angels for two minor leaguers (one named Tom Brunansky) and $100,000. As a continuation of Griffith's liquidation, catcher Butch Wynegar and pitcher Roger Erickson were traded the next day to the Yankees. Fans were upset, and players were angry. Some were very outspoken about it, even calling for the owner to be traded. The Twins had the worst attendance in the league that year, averaging 11,373 fans per game. The Twins finished 60–102. It was the worst record in the league and, at the time, the worst in Twins history (page 128).

> MLB AGREES TO REVENUE SHARING:

In December 1996, MLB players and owners agreed to a labor contract called a Collective Bargaining Agreement (CBA). This CBA included a revenue-sharing plan in lieu of a salary cap. The teams that made the most money would share their profits with the teams that made the least. The goal was to create a "level playing field" by giving all teams an opportunity to compete for the best players with the biggest contracts.

Unfortunately, teams that received revenue didn't necessarily use their profits on players' salaries. (This was addressed to some extent in a later CBA, which required each team to use the shared revenue "in an effort to improve its performance on the field." It fell short of specifying exactly what that meant.) The CBA created a system of *haves* and *have-nots* between the larger- and smaller-market teams. The Minnesota Twins are considered a small-market team in terms of revenue. Since the Twins last won a World Series in 1991, only a few small-market teams have won championships—and only one had a payroll in the bottom half of the league: the 2003 Florida Marlins. Since 1996, the Twins' total player payrolls have consistently ranked in the bottom half of the league (with a few exceptions).

> NISHIOKA'S DISAPPOINTMENT:

On November 26, 2010, the Twins paid $5.3 million for the rights to negotiate with standout Japanese infielder Tsuyoshi Nishioka. He soon signed a three-year, $9.25 million deal, making him the first Japanese-born player to join the Twins. A week into his first season, Nishioka broke his leg while trying to turn a double play. He returned in June and finished the season with a .226 batting average and only five extra-base hits. In 2012, Nishioka struggled in spring training and started the season in the minor leagues. He played in just three games for the Twins that season and went 0–14 at the plate. On September 28, 2012, Nishioka asked for and was granted his release. He gave back $3.25 million of his salary and issued an apology for his poor play. He said, "I take full responsibility for my performance, which was below my own expectations."

CHAPTER 5
PURPLE HAZE

On January 28, 1960, the NFL granted Minnesota a franchise, which would begin play in 1961. The team was named the Vikings on September 27, and that's where it all began. I used to have a sign behind my desk that read, "Would the person who left their 11 kids at the Metrodome please come pick them up? They're beating the Vikings 14–0." Someone commented, "A true Vikings fan wouldn't have a sign like that." I responded, "Only a true Vikings fan would understand it." Our Vikings team is the undisputed king of Minnesota sports heartbreak. They were the first to lose four Super Bowls. They followed that by going 0–6 in NFC championships over the next 30-plus years. The Vikings have a knack for getting our hopes up, then ripping our hearts out. But we love them anyway.

DEFENSIVE END JIM MARSHALL RUNS THE WRONG WAY

 October 25, 1964   HEARTBREAK RATING:

WHAT HAPPENED:

Just before our inaugural 1961 season, the Minnesota Vikings made a trade with the Cleveland Browns for defensive end Jim Marshall. He played well in his first three seasons with the Vikings—with 10 fumble recoveries, one of which he returned for a touchdown.

In 1964, the Vikings started the season with a respectable record of 3–3. On October 25, we faced off against the 49ers at Kezar Stadium in San Francisco. In the second half, Marshall caused a fumble that defensive end Carl Eller returned for a 45-yard touchdown. The play gave Minnesota a 27–17 lead. In the fourth quarter, San Francisco receiver Billy Kilmer caught a pass at the 49ers' 27-yard line. As he fought for extra yards, he fumbled. The ball bounced forward to the 34-yard line, where Jim Marshall scooped it up. His momentum carried him forward, and he just kept running . . . in the wrong direction. He didn't hear his teammates yelling at him to turn around. He noticed them running down the sideline, but he thought they were cheering him on. He ran 66 yards into the end zone and threw the ball toward the bleachers, believing he had scored a touchdown. The referees awarded San Francisco a safety

Jim Marshall bent down in shame after returning a fumble to the wrong end zone.

for two points. The 49ers' Bruce Bosley approached Marshall, patted his back, and said, "Thanks, Jim." After Marshall realized what had happened, he walked back to the sideline with his head down, demoralized. The 49ers added a field goal, but the Vikings held on to win, 27–22.

> WHY IT HURT SO MUCH:

When we think about our beloved Vikings' misfortune, this play is among the first to come to mind. It ranked first in NFL Films' 100 greatest follies and number 54 in the NFL's 100 greatest plays of all time. Marshall was an excellent player, who enjoyed a long and productive NFL career. Sadly, this is what many fans around the league remember most about him.

> THE AFTERMATH:

On the way home, Marshall's teammates joked that he should fly the plane, so maybe they'd end up in Hawaii. Once back in Minnesota, Marshall was swept into a media storm. He said that he couldn't fall asleep until 5 a.m. An hour later, his phone started ringing. True to our nature, Minnesota fans tried to console him. Still, Marshall felt terrible about the play and wished it never happened. That victory over the 49ers helped the Vikings earn a winning record for the first time in team history. We finished second in the NFL West at 8–5–1. Marshall played in 302 consecutive games over 20 NFL seasons, and he played in every one of the Vikings' first 290 games. He set the NFL record for most opponents' fumbles recovered (29). Marshall retired after the 1979 season, and he remains one of the greatest players in Minnesota Vikings history.

STAR QUARTERBACK FRAN TARKENTON GETS TRADED

 March 7, 1967   HEARTBREAK RATING: ♥♥♥♥♡

WHAT HAPPENED:

Head coach Norm Van Brocklin was not a fan of quarterback Fran Tarkenton's scrambling style of play. Van Brocklin wasn't alone; many experts doubted that a scrambling quarterback could ever win a championship. On November 20, 1966, Van Brocklin started Ron Vander Kelen over Tarkenton in a 21–6 loss. Two weeks later, backup quarterback Bob Berry played at quarterback—and threw five interceptions in a 20–13 defeat. Tarkenton was hurt by this, but Van Brocklin claimed he just wanted to give the other quarterbacks some experience. The Vikings finished the season at 4–9–1.

In January 1967, rumors began to circulate that Tarkenton was going to get traded. When Tarkenton heard about the rumors, he met with Van Brocklin. After their six-hour meeting, it appeared that Van Brocklin and Tarkenton had resolved their issues. But on February 10, in a sudden turn of events, Tarkenton informed the Vikings via letter that he would no longer play for the team and asked to be traded. Van Brocklin resigned the next day. Tarkenton never rescinded his demand and was traded on March 7 to the New York Giants.

Fran Tarkenton was the NFL
MVP of the 1975 season.

> WHY IT HURT SO MUCH:

In less than 30 days, we lost our starting quarterback and our head coach. Fans were understandably concerned about the direction of the franchise. One player called the situation a "mess." Tarkenton was the best quarterback in Vikings history and a future hall-of-famer. We managed to bench him, humiliate him, alienate him, and then trade him.

> THE AFTERMATH:

A few weeks after Tarkenton was traded, Bud Grant became the new head coach (page 180). In Grant's second year, our Vikings won their first division title. In his third year, the Vikings advanced to Super Bowl IV (page 38). Tarkenton played five seasons in New York. While his team never made the playoffs, he was selected to four Pro Bowls. On January 27, 1972, the Vikings traded two draft picks and three players to bring Tarkenton back to Minnesota. Grant and Tarkenton, along with the "Purple People Eaters" defense, propelled the Vikings to three more Super Bowls during the 1970s. Tarkenton was the NFL's MVP in 1975, and he was a nine-time Pro Bowl selection. When he retired in 1979, he led the league in numerous passing categories, including touchdowns, passing yards, and wins by a quarterback. In 1986, he was the first Minnesota Viking inducted into the Professional Football Hall of Fame. Grant's Vikings teams had a 158–96–5 record, won 11 division titles, and played in four Super Bowls. He retired twice, once in 1983 and again in 1985 (page 152). He was inducted into the Pro Football Hall of Fame in 1994.

NFC CHAMPIONSHIP: MINNESOTA VS. DALLAS

 January 1, 1978   HEARTBREAK RATING:

> WHAT HAPPENED:

In 1977, quarterback Fran Tarkenton was in his 17th season. The Vikings were 5–3 heading into a matchup with the Cincinnati Bengals. The Vikings led the Bengals, 21–10, when tragedy struck. Tarkenton got hit by defensive end Gary Burley and broke his ankle, as well as his thumb. The Vikings won the game, 42–10, but Tarkenton said that he had played his last NFL game.

The Vikings finished the season at 9–5 and won the division title. In the playoffs, we beat the Los Angeles Rams in a "mud bowl," 14–7. In the NFC Championship, Minnesota faced off against the Dallas Cowboys. Dallas rookie Tony Dorsett had run for 1,007 yards and 12 touchdowns that season, and the Cowboys led the league in offensive yards. The Dallas defense ranked first in fewest yards allowed. The Cowboys were favored by 11.5 points.

As was the story for most of the season, our defense played well, but our offense couldn't get going. Dorsett and fellow running back Robert Newhouse led the Dallas rushing attack with a combined 152 yards and two touchdowns. The Dallas

defense sacked quarterback Bob Lee twice and intercepted him once. They also stuffed the Vikings' running game and forced two fumbles by star running back Chuck Foreman. For as much as our offense struggled, we only trailed 16–6 with seven minutes left in the game. However, a fumbled punt was recovered by Dallas and set up a Dorsett touchdown run. The Cowboys beat the Vikings, 23–6. They went on to win Super Bowl XII, 27–10, over the Denver Broncos.

> WHY IT HURT SO MUCH:

Being one game away from the Super Bowl and losing is almost as heartbreaking as getting there and blowing it. This one was a bit heavier on the heart because it marked the end of an era. Our Vikings team, which once was young and full of promise, was now showing its age. Fans and players had to face the fact that it was time to rebuild; the Super Bowl window had closed. This had been the last chance for our "Purple People Eaters" to win a Super Bowl.

> THE AFTERMATH:

Tarkenton came back for one more year in 1978 and led the team to another division title. The Vikings lost in the divisional round to the Los Angeles Rams, 34–10. Tarkenton took a job broadcasting with ABC. Center Mick Tingelhoff also retired. In the years that followed, the Vikings said goodbye to such greats as Carl Eller, Chuck Foreman, Paul Krause, Jim Marshall, and Ron Yary. Minnesota went 0–5 in NFC championship games after the loss to the Cowboys in 1978.

VIKINGS BLOW CHANCE TO PROMOTE BUDDY RYAN

 February 28, 1978   HEARTBREAK RATING:

WHAT HAPPENED:

Jim Finks was the general manager of the Minnesota Vikings from 1964 to 1974. He is largely credited with building the Vikings into a defensive power in the 1970s. In May 1974, he resigned because he was interested in a higher position with a team and possibly an ownership opportunity. There were also rumors that he didn't get along with Vikings team president Max Winter. In September 1974, Finks was hired by the Chicago Bears as general manager and team president. Finks wanted to build the Bears into a defensive force. The Vikings' defensive coordinator during most of the "Purple People Eaters" era was Neill Armstrong (1971–1977). After Minnesota lost to Dallas in the 1977 NFC Championship (page 146), Finks hired Armstrong as the Bears' head coach. The speculation was that our defensive line coach Buddy Ryan might follow Armstrong to Chicago, unless the Vikings promoted him to defensive coordinator.

On February 28, 1978, *The Minneapolis Tribune*'s Sid Hartman reported that the Vikings were looking outside the organization for a new defensive coordinator. That same day, Ryan accepted the defensive coordinator position with the Chicago Bears. Armstrong was fired after four seasons. Ryan, however, was

offered a contract extension and was willing to work under new head coach Mike Ditka. Ryan created a formidable defensive scheme called the "46 defense." In the 1985 season, the Bears went 15–1 and defeated the New England Patriots in Super Bowl XX, 46–10, largely on the strength of Ryan's defense. That defense is considered one of the best—if not the very best—defenses of all time.

> WHY IT HURT SO MUCH:

Coaches get plucked from other teams' staffs every year, but not promoting them when you have a chance is another story. It's hard to say what would've happened if Ryan had become our defensive coordinator. Yet he was far from the only former Vikings coach to win a Super Bowl elsewhere. On one hand, we're happy for them; on the other, we're jealous and wonder why we didn't keep them. If we had won a Super Bowl along the way, few would question those decisions. But it's disheartening that we didn't win a championship, while former coordinators like Brian Billick, Tony Dungy, and Mike Tomlin did.

> THE AFTERMATH:

When Finks left the Vikings, Mike Lynn was hired as an assistant to Winter. Lynn was eventually named general manager. Finks resigned from the Bears in 1983, at least in part because owner George Halas hired Ditka without consulting him. Finks went on to work for the Chicago Cubs and the New Orleans Saints. He was elected to the Pro Football Hall of Fame in 1995. Ryan was the head coach of the Philadelphia Eagles from 1986 through 1990. He coached the Arizona Cardinals in 1994 and 1995.

FINAL GAME AT MET STADIUM TURNS INTO DESTRUCTIVE RIOT

 December 20, 1981   HEARTBREAK RATING:

WHAT HAPPENED:

Metropolitan Stadium in Bloomington, Minnesota, opened on April 24, 1956. It was the home of the Minnesota Twins and the Minnesota Vikings, as well as the Minnesota Kicks soccer team and the Minneapolis Millers baseball team for the first few years. The "Met," an outdoor stadium, gave the Vikings a distinct advantage because of the cold weather. Yet on December 1, 1978, the Metropolitan Sports Facilities Commission voted to construct a domed stadium in downtown Minneapolis.

The last year of operation for the Met would be 1981, which meant that the last game played in the stadium would be on December 20, when the Vikings hosted the Kansas City Chiefs— unless Minnesota qualified for the postseason. Unfortunately, a four-game losing streak late in the year all but eliminated us from playoff contention. When the New York Giants beat the Dallas Cowboys on December 19, the Vikings were officially out of the playoff race.

The next day was the final game ever played at Metropolitan Stadium. The game itself was dull compared to what followed. Minnesota fell, 10–6, and only scored on two Rick Danmeier

field goals. With five minutes left in the game, fans started to tear the stadium apart—eventually climbing on the scoreboard, ripping out light bulbs and wires, and causing the clock to stop permanently on 3:10. In a riotous attempt to claim souvenirs, they pulled up seats and benches, and they took down goal posts. Some fans even brought power tools to help them secure their keepsakes. Fans went so far as to steal urinals, which caused flooding. Even though there were 50 police offers inside the stadium (a typical game normally garnered 10–12 officers), law enforcement was severely outnumbered. Officers had to use mace on fans who refused to leave the field.

> WHY IT HURT SO MUCH:

In an effort to preserve a piece of the stadium, fans crossed the line from nostalgia to vandalism, showing us a glimpse at the darker side of human behavior. Harry Randolph, the stadium ticket manager said, "There is certain sentiment in trying to take a seat home, but people climbing the scoreboard are sick. They endanger themselves."

> THE AFTERMATH:

Amazingly, no one was seriously hurt. Only one injury required hospitalization: An individual was struck with a board. Nine people were treated at local hospitals for minor injuries, and many others were treated at the Met. One man was arrested, and eight others were given citations for trespassing or disorderly conduct. Demolition of the stadium began on January 28, 1985, and lasted four months. The site is now the home of the famed Mall of America.

LES STECKEL LEADS THE VIKINGS TO A 3-13 RECORD

 December 17, 1984   HEARTBREAK RATING:

 WHAT HAPPENED:

In 1983, Minnesota Vikings head coach Bud Grant missed the playoffs for only the fifth time in his 17 seasons with the team. Vikings management wondered if Grant had perhaps lost his passion for coaching. On January 27, 1984, Grant resigned. He said that he was not pressured and just felt the time was right. Vikings team president Max Winter and general manager Mike Lynn met with Grant. They decided to promote wide receivers coach Les Steckel to become the third head coach in franchise history. Steckel had never been a head coach before, but the team thought he would get more out of the players—and he had potential to be a long-term head coach.

Steckel reportedly ran training camp like a military base. Some players collapsed and several other players were injured. Steckel felt that the team was in rebuilding mode. He cut a few veterans at the end of training camp, and during the season, he waived and traded others, which angered the team. Many players grew frustrated with Steckel. Some believed that he was trying to control their personal lives, and some felt that he was trying to impose his religious beliefs upon them.

In the season opener, the Vikings lost to the San Diego Chargers, 42–13. It was the worst opening day loss in franchise history. Midway through the season, offensive coordinator Jerry Burns announced that he would resign after the season; Steckel had taken over most of his duties, and Burns no longer felt useful. By the end of November, Lynn seemed to realize that Steckel had lost control of the team. On December 8, the Vikings fell to the San Francisco 49ers, 51–7, the worst blowout in team history. We finished the season at 3–13, the worst record in team history. On December 17, Lynn asked for Steckel's resignation. The head coach refused to resign and was fired.

> WHY IT HURT SO MUCH:

Up until that season, the Vikings were viewed as one of the best franchises in the league. Lynn felt that the team had quickly become a laughingstock and that the team's image had been tarnished. Some players felt that Steckel wasn't the only one to blame and that some of the damage reflected upon Lynn.

> THE AFTERMATH:

Management learned their lesson. Almost immediately after firing Steckel, Lynn convinced Grant to return. The day after Steckel was fired, Grant signed a lifetime contract with the Vikings that was renewable on a year-to-year basis. It gave him the choice to retire whenever he wanted. Grant led the 1985 Vikings to a 7–9 record, which was viewed as a success because of the improvement in play, personnel, and attitude. On January 6, 1986, Grant announced his retirement, and the Vikings introduced Jerry Burns as the new head coach.

NFC CHAMPIONSHIP: MINNESOTA VS. WASHINGTON

 January 17, 1988   HEARTBREAK RATING: 💔💔💔💔💔

> WHAT HAPPENED:

In 1987, the Minnesota Vikings' 8–7 record was enough to earn a wildcard berth in the playoffs. Because the team finished the regular season by losing three out of four games, most experts felt that the Vikings didn't stand a chance in the postseason. We faced the New Orleans Saints on January 3, 1988. The Saints had the second-best record in the league at 12–3, and they started the wildcard game fast, jumping to a 7–0 lead. But Minnesota's star wide receiver Anthony Carter returned a punt 84 yards for a touchdown, which seemed to awaken the Vikings. Our underdogs went on to win in blowout fashion, 44–10. Next, the Vikings traveled to San Francisco to face the NFL's top team, the 49ers (13–2). The home team was favored by 11 points, but Carter had a record-breaking day, catching 10 passes for 227 yards. Minnesota shocked San Francisco, 36–24.

The Vikings advanced to the NFC Championship, on the road against the Washington Redskins on January 17. The defensive battle yielded a tie game, 10–10, in the fourth quarter. Washington quarterback Doug Williams completed a touchdown pass to receiver Gary Clark, giving his team a 17–10 advantage. In the final minutes, Vikings quarterback Wade Wilson led the Vikings

Darrin Nelson led the NFL with 4.9 yards per carry in 1987.

on a drive to Washington's six-yard line. On fourth down, with a minute left, Wilson threw a short pass to running back Darrin Nelson at the goal line. The ball hit Nelson in the hands. A catch might have been a touchdown. At worst, it would have created a first down, just a few inches from the end zone. But Nelson dropped the pass. It was one of eight dropped passes by Vikings receivers on the day. Washington won, 17–10.

> WHY IT HURT SO MUCH:

The Twins won the World Series a few months earlier and had traveled a similar path, beating heavily favored teams along the way. Minnesotans felt like the sports gods were smiling down on us. When the magic ran out, it hurt. Vikings fans look back on that play as one of the biggest "what ifs" in team history.

> THE AFTERMATH:

The Redskins went on to win Super Bowl XXII, 42–10, over the Denver Broncos. In 1988, the Vikings finished the regular season with an 11–5 record. In the playoffs, we beat the Los Angeles Rams, 28–17, but lost in the divisional round to the 49ers, 34–9.

> DAN'S NOTES:

On the same day as Nelson's drop, Cleveland Browns running back Earnest Byner lost a fumble at the goal line with 1:12 to go in the AFC Championship. Had Byner scored, it would have tied the game (assuming the extra point was good). Instead, Denver took a safety and won, 38–33. This is one of many examples of Minnesota and Cleveland sports teams having a strange cosmic connection in heartbreak.

QUARTERBACK EMBARRASSES VIKINGS DEFENSE . . . ON A RUN

 October 30, 1988   HEARTBREAK RATING:

> WHAT HAPPENED:

What do the following Minnesota Vikings have in common: Joey Browner, Brad Edwards, Carl Lee, Chris Martin, Keith Millard, Jesse Solomon—and Joey Browner again? Those are the names of our defenders who *almost* tackled San Francisco 49ers quarterback Steve Young on his famous 49-yard, game-winning touchdown run. The two teams met in Week 9 of the 1988 season. San Francisco's legendary quarterback (and future hall-of-famer) Joe Montana had injured his back in practice. So backup quarterback (and future hall-of-famer) Steve Young started instead. Vikings head coach Jerry Burns was well aware of Young's running ability and said before the game, ". . . we'll have to be sure to contain him."

The Vikings held a 21–17 lead late in the fourth quarter, but the 49ers offense had one last chance. It was third down and two yards to go at the Vikings' 49-yard line. With about two minutes left in the game, Young took the snap under center. He dropped back to pass and looked left to throw downfield. The pocket began to collapse, so he tucked the ball to protect it. He spun and escaped to his right, and he took off running. He ran down the field, then veered left and made his way to the

sideline. Several Vikings defenders missed the quarterback or were blocked out of his way at the last instant. Young tripped and almost fell at the 10-yard line, but he stumbled toward the goal line, and his momentum carried him in for the score. The Vikings attempted to come back, but the drive stalled at midfield. The 49ers won, 24–21.

> WHY IT HURT SO MUCH:

It feels almost typical for our Vikings to let a game slip away at the last second in dramatic fashion. That play still haunts us—and it was shown on television *all the time*. As a child, I remember thinking, "Why does it seem like the other teams' greatest plays and highlights are always against us?"

> THE AFTERMATH:

The Vikings finished the season at 11–5, one game behind the Chicago Bears (12–4), which earned us a wildcard berth. After winning our first playoff game, we were trounced by the 49ers—this time with Montana—by a score of 34–9. The 49ers went on to win Super Bowl XXIII over the Cincinnati Bengals.

> DAN'S NOTES:

In 1984, Young was given a $40 million contract to play in the United States Football League. Vikings general manager Mike Lynn called it the "craziest, dumbest, and poorest business deal" that he could recall. Ironically, five years later, Lynn traded for Herschel Walker (page 34), which just might be the craziest, dumbest, and poorest business deal in the history of the NFL.

NFC CHAMPIONSHIP: MINNESOTA VS. NEW YORK

 January 14, 2001   HEARTBREAK RATING:

> WHAT HAPPENED:

In 2000, quarterback Jeff George left Minnesota and signed with the Washington Redskins. The Vikings also released quarterback Randall Cunningham. We tried to lure future hall-of-famer Dan Marino to Minnesota, but he retired instead. That opened the door for second-year quarterback Daunte Culpepper. For the season, he averaged 246 yards passing per game and threw 33 touchdowns. More importantly, he led the Vikings to an 11–5 record and the NFC Central Division title. In the playoffs, Minnesota defeated the New Orleans Saints, 34–16, to advance to the NFC Championship versus the New York Giants on January 14, 2001, at Giants Stadium.

The Giants had a reputation as a running team, and the Vikings' defensive scheme was planned around that. On the first series of the game, New York quarterback Kerry Collins threw a 46-yard touchdown pass. On the ensuing kickoff, Vikings running back Moe Williams fumbled, which led to another touchdown pass by Collins. The Vikings offense just couldn't get going, and the defense had no answer for Collins. He threw four touchdowns in the first half, and his team built a 34–0 lead.

For the Vikings offense, it was more of the same in the second half. But New York's offense mercifully took their foot off the accelerator. Collins threw a touchdown pass in the third quarter, and that ended the day's scoring. Minnesota lost 41–0 (or 41–donut, as Vikings fans call it). Collins finished with 381 yards passing and five touchdowns. Culpepper tallied just 78 yards and threw three interceptions.

> WHY IT HURT SO MUCH:

Would you rather have loved and lost, or never loved at all? Before the season, most fans would be happy if their team made it to the NFC Championship. But for Minnesota fans, this was the hump we couldn't get over. Not only was this another NFC Championship loss, it felt like our team didn't even show up. This was the most lopsided loss and the only shutout in Vikings playoff history.

> THE AFTERMATH:

There was speculation that the Giants may have been stealing the Vikings' play signals, and there were rumors that the NFL might investigate, but nothing ever materialized. Following the season, running back Robert Smith unexpectedly retired. After trying to renegotiate defensive tackle John Randle's contract, the Vikings released him in March. He spent three seasons in Seattle before retiring and was elected to the Pro Football Hall of Fame in 2010. Head coach Denny Green was bought out of his contract before the end of the following season. Minnesota would not reach the NFC Championship again until the 2009 NFL season (page 48).

MINNESOTA VIKINGS DON'T DRAFT A PLAYER IN TIME, TWICE

 April 2002–April 2003   HEARTBREAK RATING:

> WHAT HAPPENED:

The Minnesota Vikings have a history of conflict within the front office. In 1974, future hall-of-fame general manager Jim Finks resigned because he reportedly didn't get along with team president Max Winter. In the 1980s, Mike Lynn and Winter battled over control of the team, which ended with Winter selling his shares of the team and leaving the board of directors in 1989. Head coach Denny Green wrote a book in 1997 called *No Room for Crybabies*. In it, he discussed a plan to sue ownership over an alleged plot to oust him and hire Lou Holtz.

In 2002, Frank Gilliam was put in charge of football operations. On April 20, the Vikings hoped to draft defensive tackle Ryan Sims from the University of North Carolina with the seventh overall pick. The Dallas Cowboys, just ahead of the Vikings, were negotiating a trade with the Kansas City Chiefs when time ran out on them. The Vikings could've jumped in and nabbed Sims—but we didn't move quickly enough. Before we got our draft card to the podium, the trade was finalized. Kansas City picked Sims; the Vikings chose offensive tackle Bryant McKinnie. Vikings owner Red McCombs was reportedly upset about what happened, and Gilliam was demoted to talent evaluator.

In his 13-year career, Kevin Williams totaled 63 sacks.

In the following year's draft, the Vikings once again had issues getting our draft card to the podium in time. On April 26, 2003, the Vikings were slotted to have the seventh overall pick but ran out of time while negotiating a trade with Baltimore. Jacksonville and Carolina quickly took advantage of the Vikings' misstep. Both teams made their selections ahead of the Vikings. Jacksonville chose quarterback Byron Leftwich, and Carolina picked offensive tackle Jordan Gross. The Vikings slipped down two spots and ended up selecting ninth. We chose defensive tackle Kevin Williams from Oklahoma State—and claimed that we got the player we wanted anyway.

> WHY IT HURT SO MUCH:

By not getting a draft card to the podium in time—two years in a row—it suggested a certain amount of ineptitude, and it left fans doubting our team's leadership. Even if Kevin Williams was the guy we wanted, we probably could've traded down and gotten extra draft picks to go with him.

> THE AFTERMATH:

Despite the draft disasters, everything worked out for us. Sims was considered a bust in Kansas City, while McKinnie spent nine years with the Vikings. He showed flashes of greatness but was inconsistent. Williams played with Minnesota for 11 seasons; he was a five-time All-Pro and a six-time Pro Bowl selection. Gilliam stayed with the Vikings organization until 2007 and was credited for finding late-round draft steals like Brad Johnson (QB) and Scott Studwell (LB).

CARDINALS KNOCK VIKINGS OUT OF THE PLAYOFFS—"NO!"

 December 28, 2003   HEARTBREAK RATING: ♥♥♥♥♥

 WHAT HAPPENED:

The Minnesota Vikings started the 2003 season by winning our first six games. We followed that with a four-game losing streak; three of those losses came to teams with a combined record of 5–18. By the final week of the regular season, we were tied with the Green Bay Packers for first place in the NFC North at 9–6. The Vikings played the 3–12 Arizona Cardinals in Tempe, Arizona, and were 7.5-point favorites. All we had to do was win the game, and we would be division champions. A loss would knock us out of the playoffs—because Green Bay routed the Denver Broncos (who rested their key players), 31–3.

Minnesota controlled most of the game and held a 17–6 lead midway through the fourth quarter. But Cardinals quarterback Josh McCown constructed a 15-play drive that resulted in a two-yard touchdown pass to tight end Steve Bush. After a failed attempt at a two-point conversion, the Cardinals trailed 17–12 with two minutes to go. Victory still seemed likely for the Vikings—until the ensuing kickoff. Instead of booting the ball deep, the Cardinals tried an onside kick and recovered the football at their 39-yard line. Arizona marched to the nine-yard line before the Vikings defense finally woke up. Our team

sacked McCown on second and goal, back to the 17-yard line. On third down, we sacked him again and caused a fumble, which the Cardinals recovered at the 28-yard line.

Arizona was out of timeouts. The game's final seconds were ticking away. They were 28 yards from the end zone. It would take a miracle for Minnesota to lose. The Cardinals hurried to the line of scrimmage and snapped the ball with four seconds on the clock. McCown dropped back to pass, stepped up in the pocket, then ran to his right. He heaved a pass to the back corner of the end zone. It was caught by receiver Nate Poole for the game-winning touchdown. Poole only got one foot in bounds, but the referees ruled that he was forced out. The play was reviewed and confirmed. The Cardinals won, 18–17.

> WHY IT HURT SO MUCH:

"No! No! The Cardinals have knocked the Vikings out of the playoffs!" Those were the immortal words of Vikings radio announcer Paul Allen. He spoke for all of us fans. Blowing an 11-point lead with less than seven minutes to go felt so . . . Minnesota sports. This was one of those moments when we couldn't help but think, *Why does this keep happening to us?*

> THE AFTERMATH:

The Packers finished 10–6 and won the division. The Vikings became the first 6–0 team to wind up missing the playoffs since 1990, when the league adopted its 12-team playoff format. In other words, it was the biggest regular-season collapse in the history of the NFL. (The Denver Broncos matched it in 2009.)

MINNESOTA VIKINGS TRADE RANDY MOSS TO OAKLAND

 March 2, 2005   HEARTBREAK RATING:

> WHAT HAPPENED:

The Minnesota Vikings selected Randy Moss in the 1998 NFL Draft. Because of his troubled past, the top-10 talent slid down to us at pick number 21. In his first seven seasons, Moss was named first-team All-Pro three times and was selected to five Pro Bowls. He was arguably the best receiver in the league. But several incidents tarnished his reputation. In the 1999 season, he was fined for verbally abusing a side judge in one game and for squirting a referee with a water bottle in another. In 2000, he was fined for making contact with an official, and in 2001, Moss verbally abused corporate sponsors on the team bus because they were sitting where he wanted to sit. He was fined again and required to attend anger management classes. Moss was sometimes criticized for not giving 100% effort during games. When asked about it, he infamously declared, "I play when I want to play."

On September 24, 2002, Moss was arrested for contacting and pushing a traffic officer down the street with his car. He was charged with misdemeanors for careless driving and failure to obey an officer. He was also charged with marijuana possession a week later. At the end of the 2004 season, the Vikings lost

Randy Moss led the NFL in receiving
touchdowns five different times.

a close game to Washington, 21–18. Frustrated, Moss went to the locker room before the end of the game. A week later, after scoring a touchdown in Green Bay, Moss pretended to moon the fans and then wipe his rear end on the goal post. On March 2, 2005, Moss was traded to the Oakland Raiders for linebacker Napoleon Harris, a first-round pick, and a seventh-round pick.

> WHY IT HURT SO MUCH:

Moss may have been the most talented receiver that ever played. He was certainly someone who could've helped the Vikings win. It's too bad his (first) stint had to end the way it did.

> THE AFTERMATH:

The Vikings used the first-round draft pick from Oakland to select Moss's replacement: wide receiver Troy Williamson (page 178). Harris was with the Vikings for three seasons. Moss spent two disappointing seasons in Oakland and was traded to New England. There, he had a record-breaking 2007 season in which he caught 23 touchdowns. His Patriots went 16–0 but lost Super Bowl XLI. He was traded back to Minnesota in 2010 (page 171).

> DAN'S NOTES:

I've coached enough to know how a player's poor attitude can affect the rest of the team. Sometimes, addition by subtraction can be an effective strategy to improve a team's success, as well as morale. It's sad that it had to end that way. Back then, I believed he wasn't worth the trouble. Having said that, I look back now and wonder . . . *What was I thinking?*

VIKINGS PLAYERS GET INTO TROUBLE ON THE "LOVE BOAT"

 October 6, 2005 HEARTBREAK RATING:

> WHAT HAPPENED:

The Minnesota Vikings' 2005 was tumultuous. Randy Moss was traded (page 166), Onterrio Smith was suspended (page 182), and Troy Williamson was drafted (page 178). Head coach Mike Tice got into trouble for scalping Super Bowl tickets. Near the end of May, owner Red McCombs sold the team. Zygi, Mark, and Leonard Wilf officially took over as owners in mid-June.

The Vikings started the season 1–3 and then went into the bye week. Defensive back Fred Smoot was put in charge of a traditional rookie party, held during the bye week each year. Smoot and defensive end Lance Johnstone reserved two luxury charter boats on Lake Minnetonka, southwest of Minneapolis. On October 6, several exotic dancers and 30 players were driven to the lake in a caravan of limousines. One of the limos reportedly stopped to allow players to urinate on someone's lawn. The property owner followed the limousines to Lake Minnetonka and then called the police.

The police were again called at 7:30 p.m. by a boat employee who reported "possible prostitution, drugs, and sex acts." Other employees later said they "had to step around people

who were having sex on the floor." According to reports, players became verbally abusive to some of the bartenders and began asking some of the waitstaff to "dance." Workers aboard the boat no longer felt safe. After radioing to shore, the crew was told to return to the dock. The scheduled 3.5-hour cruise lasted about 40 minutes. As news of the incident got out, the scandal was infamously nicknamed the "Love Boat."

> WHY IT HURT SO MUCH:

Not every player on board acted inappropriately, and not every team member was there. But the situation reflected poorly on the team. The Vikings' reputation was already a bit tarnished due to players and their legal problems—and the organization was making a push with the state legislature for a new stadium and had recently unveiled plans for the project.

> THE AFTERMATH:

On October 14, Zygi Wilf apologized and vowed to "build a first-class franchise." On December 15, charges were filed against Smoot, Daunte Culpepper (QB), Bryant McKinnie (OT), and Moe Williams (RB) for misdemeanor disorderly conduct. On January 1, 2006, the Vikings beat the Chicago Bears, 34–10, in the season's final game. Wilf fired Tice 20 minutes later. On March 14, the Vikings traded Culpepper to the Miami Dolphins, and on April 4, charges against him were dropped. (Smoot later said that Culpepper "did nothing" and "acted tastefully through the whole night.") On April 20, Williams was found guilty. The team did not re-sign him. On May 26, Smoot and McKinnie pled guilty. They both returned for the 2006 season.

VIKINGS TRADE FOR RANDY MOSS ... THEN RELEASE HIM

 October 6, 2010   HEARTBREAK RATING: ♥♥♥♡♡

 WHAT HAPPENED:

Star wide receiver Randy Moss was traded out of Minnesota in 2005 (page 166). In 2010, he was in the final year of his contract with the New England Patriots. Early in September, the Patriots held a Charitable Foundation Kickoff Gala. Players sat at tables and socialized with people who had donated large amounts of money. Instead of sitting at his assigned table with guests who paid to sit with him, Moss sat at a table alone, wearing headphones and listening to music. A week and a half later, after an opening day victory against the Cincinnati Bengals, Moss openly talked to reporters about not getting a contract extension. He said that he felt like he wasn't appreciated.

In Minnesota, the Vikings' leading receiver from the previous season, Sidney Rice, was recovering from surgery. On October 6, we sent a third-round draft pick to New England and brought Moss back to the team. At his re-introductory press conference Moss said that he was "back home." Over the next three games, Moss caught 12 passes for 166 yards and two touchdowns. The Vikings went 1–2. Our next game was against the Patriots. Two days before the matchup against his former team, Moss lashed out at caterers in the Vikings locker room. He reportedly said

that he "wouldn't feed this to [his] [expletive] dog." The Vikings fell to the Patriots, 28–18, and Moss caught just one pass for eight yards. After the game, he reportedly told Vikings owner Zygi Wilf that head coach Brad Childress wasn't a good coach and should be fired. During his post-game press conference, Moss got emotional and discussed how much he missed the Patriots. He went on to criticize the Vikings. The following day, November 1, Childress met with the team and informed them that he was cutting Moss. Wilf was reportedly upset because he had not been informed—Childress had apparently released Moss without the owner's consent.

> WHY IT HURT SO MUCH:

After a heartbreaking loss in the NFC Championship Game the previous season (page 48), hopes were high in 2010. When Moss joined the team, fans felt like maybe we could put together another magical run. With some of the best players in NFL history—Brett Favre, Adrian Peterson, and Moss—on the same roster, how could we go wrong? But Moss seemed to fall back into his old antics, and the Vikings wanted no part of it. We finished the season a disappointing 6–10.

> THE AFTERMATH:

Moss was placed on waivers and was claimed by the Tennessee Titans. He played in eight games with Tennessee, catching six passes for 80 yards. He retired in 2011 but played with the San Francisco 49ers in 2012; his team fell to the Baltimore Ravens in Super Bowl XLVII by a score of 34–31. He was inducted into the Pro Football Hall of Fame in 2018.

BLAIR WALSH MISSES GAME-WINNING PLAYOFF KICK

 January 10, 2016   HEARTBREAK RATING:

> WHAT HAPPENED:

Minnesota Vikings kicker Gary Anderson notoriously missed a field goal in the 1998 NFC Championship (page 50). Since then, kicker mishaps have seemingly become part of our team's identity. In 2002, Doug Brien missed four out of five field goals during the preseason. Then, in Week 2, he missed a field goal and two extra points. The Vikings lost in overtime, 45–39. Brien was released a few weeks later.

In 2012, the Vikings used a sixth-round pick to draft a kicker from the University of Georgia named Blair Walsh. In his rookie season, he led the league in field goals and was named first-team All-Pro. In the years that followed, he had his ups and downs. In 2014, he was the NFL's least accurate kicker. But in 2015, Walsh once again led the league in field goals with 34. The Vikings finished the season at 11–5 and hosted the Seattle Seahawks in a wildcard playoff game on January 10, 2016.

The game was held outdoors at TCF Bank Stadium because the Vikings' new stadium was still being built. The temperature that day was -6 degrees with a wind chill of -25. Minnesota dominated for three quarters but only had three field goals to

In 2012, Blair Walsh was
first-team All-Pro.

show for it. The Seahawks cut the Vikings' lead to 9–7 early in the fourth. On Minnesota's next possession, running back Adrian Peterson fumbled away the football at the 40-yard line. Seattle moved the ball 12 yards and then kicked a go-ahead field goal. The teams traded a few punts as time ticked away. Trailing 10–9, the Vikings had one last chance to win. Quarterback Teddy Bridgewater marched the offense to Seattle's nine-yard line. There, with 26 seconds left on the clock, Walsh lined up for the game-winning 27-yard field goal. He missed. Seattle won, and the Vikings were out of the playoffs.

> WHY IT HURT SO MUCH:

This was our first playoff game in three years. It was a home game. We dramatically outplayed our opponents. (Their only scores were set up by a fluke play and a turnover.) Plus, Walsh had already hit three field goals that day—two of which were considerably longer and more difficult. Of course, almost 17 years to the day after Anderson missed his kick wide left, Walsh missed left too. This one stung in every way possible.

> THE AFTERMATH:

The following season, Walsh was released after missing four extra points in the first nine games. He spent the 2017 season with the Seahawks. On November 5, he was 0–3 on field goal attempts in a 17–14 loss. Two weeks later, he missed a last-second, game-tying kick. In Week 17, with his team trailing 26–24, in his final NFL kick, Walsh missed a game-winner with 37 seconds to go. Seattle finished 9–7 and missed the playoffs.

DANIEL CARLSON MISSES TWO FIELD GOALS . . . IN OVERTIME

 September 16, 2018   HEARTBREAK RATING:

> WHAT HAPPENED:

In the fifth round of the 2018 NFL Draft, the Minnesota Vikings used the 167th overall pick to select Daniel Carlson, kicker, from Auburn University. To quote Michael Salfino of ABC News' FiveThirtyEight, "A fifth-round pick for a kicker is more like a first-rounder for any other position." It was a gamble, but the Vikings were desperate for stability at the position.

Against the San Francisco 49ers in Week 1, Carlson made three extra-point attempts and kicked a 48-yard field goal. We won, 24–16. The following week, the Vikings traveled to Green Bay to face the Packers, our bitter division rival. Carlson missed a 48-yard field goal in the final minutes of the second quarter, and Green Bay went into halftime with a 17–7 lead. In the third quarter, the Packers added a field goal—and then the fireworks began. In the fourth quarter, Vikings quarterback Kirk Cousins threw two touchdown passes to receiver Stefon Diggs, while the Packers put two field goals on the board. Trailing 26–21, with 2:13 to go, Minnesota turned over the ball; the Packers intercepted a tipped pass. Our defense held Green Bay to another field goal and allowed just 19 seconds to run off the clock. Minnesota trailed, 29–21.

On our next offensive play, Cousins was again intercepted, essentially ending the game. But a questionable roughing-the-passer penalty against the Packers gave us another chance. The Vikings cashed in. Cousins threw his third touchdown of the quarter and added a two-point conversion, tying the game. Yet, in the final 31 seconds, the Packers drove into field-goal range. Kicker Mason Crosby appeared to hit a game-winner, but Vikings head coach Mike Zimmer had called a timeout just before the play. Crosby tried again—and missed. In overtime, we advanced to Green Bay's 31-yard line, where Carlson missed his second field goal of the day. After our defense forced a Packers' punt, Cousins once again led our team into scoring position. With the final seconds ticking away, Carlson missed a 35-yard field goal. The game ended in a tie, 29–29.

> WHY IT HURT SO MUCH:

It was Packers Week—in Green Bay—and we should've won. If Carlson had made a field goal, we'd remember this as one of the most thrilling games in Vikings' history. Instead, it's remembered as a dud.

> THE AFTERMATH:

Carlson was released the next day. When asked why, Zimmer famously replied, "Did you see the game?" A month later, Carlson signed with the Oakland Raiders. Minnesota finished 8–7–1 and missed the playoffs by half a game. In August 2019, the Vikings traded a fifth-round pick to the Baltimore Ravens for kicker/punter Kaare Vedvik. He performed poorly during the preseason and was released three weeks later.

THE VIKINGS' MEMORABLE FIRST-ROUND DRAFT BUSTS

 1999, 2005, and 2011   HEARTBREAK RATING: 🖤🖤🖤🖤🖤

> DIMITRIUS UNDERWOOD:

The Vikings selected defensive end Dimitrius Underwood from Michigan State University with the 29th pick in the NFL draft on April 17, 1999. Coaches from Michigan State had warned us about him because of possible character issues—and he was projected to be a fifth-round pick, at best. Underwood missed two flights to Minnesota, missed a few days of mini-camp, and fired multiple agents. On August 1, he reported to training camp and signed a five-year, $5.3 million contract with a $1.7 million signing bonus. After one practice, he left the facility, caught a flight to Cleveland, went to Philadelphia, and then disappeared. On August 3, he said that he wanted to return but never came. He was found on August 8. Two days later, he returned and met with head coach Denny Green. The next day, the Vikings released a statement that said Dimitrius "has no desire to play football and has decided not to play for the Vikings." Underwood returned his signing bonus. The Vikings gave him a reported $50,000 settlement and waived him.

> TROY WILLIAMSON:

On April 23, 2005, the Vikings had the seventh pick in the draft, which they had acquired from Oakland in a trade for

Randy Moss (page 166). The Vikings were looking to draft a wide receiver to replace Moss. We chose Troy Williamson from the University of South Carolina. As it turned out, Williamson was fast, but he had trouble catching the ball. In 2006, he caught 37 receptions for 455 yards, and he dropped 11 passes. It was determined that Williamson had vision issues, so he was given exercises to improve his eyesight. The exercises didn't seem to help. In the final game of the 2007 season, Williamson dropped a wide-open pass that would've been a 72-yard touchdown. On February 29, 2008, the Vikings traded Williamson to Jacksonville for a sixth-round pick.

> CHRISTIAN PONDER:

Three quarterbacks were ranked near the top of the draft board on April 28, 2011: Cam Newton, Jake Locker, and Blaine Gabbert. The Vikings were set to pick 12th and had their eyes on a quarterback of the future. But drafting a quarterback was a gamble; the wrong player could set back an organization for years. Nevertheless, Newton was the first pick of the draft. Locker went eighth, and Gabbert was chosen tenth. All three top quarterback prospects were gone. So we picked . . . Christian Ponder, quarterback, from Florida State University. Ponder was projected to be chosen late in the first round, at best. Fans at the team's draft party were stunned. Many booed. Some laughed. Ponder was with Minnesota from 2011 to 2014. He started 36 games and managed a record of 14–21–1.

Dan's Notes: It felt to many fans like our Vikings panicked and took a quarterback just to take a quarterback.

QUICK HITS: OUT OF BOUNDS

❯ VIKINGS MISS OUT ON GRANT AS HEAD COACH:

In 1960, Vikings ownership began searching for the team's first head coach. Two names emerged: Norm Van Brocklin, a former quarterback who had retired after winning the 1960 NFL championship with the Philadelphia Eagles; and Harry Peter "Bud" Grant, Jr., head coach of the Canadian Football League's Winnipeg Blue Bombers. Grant was a former three-sport athlete at the University of Minnesota. He played two seasons of professional basketball with the Minneapolis Lakers (1949–1951). Then he switched to football and played for the Eagles (1951–1952) and the Blue Bombers (1953–1956). In 1957, he became Winnipeg's head coach. Grant turned the Blue Bombers into a powerhouse, winning four championships as head coach. Vikings ownership was divided between Van Brocklin and Grant. It was reported that three owners were in favor of Van Brocklin and two wanted Grant. But Grant made the decision for them. On January 18, 1961, he informed the Vikings that he no longer wanted to be considered for the job. Later that day, Van Brocklin was named the first head coach of the Minnesota Vikings.

❯ DARRIN NELSON ASKS VIKINGS NOT TO PICK HIM:

In the 1982 NFL Draft, the Vikings were set to pick seventh. The team wanted Stanford running back Darrin Nelson. Minnesota's backup quarterback Steve Dils had played with Nelson at Stanford and told Vikings officials that Nelson was an

"explosive" player. Nelson, however, wanted nothing to do with Minnesota. He sent a letter to the Vikings asking our team not to draft him. On April 27, we drafted him anyway. Nelson told reporters he was "disappointed." When asked why he didn't feel like Minnesota was a good fit, Nelson said he was used to "big cities," and he liked going to discos. A reporter informed Nelson that the Twin Cities had discos. Nelson responded that he didn't want to go to a disco and listen to country music. In drafting Nelson, the Vikings passed on future hall-of-fame running back Marcus Allen, who was selected by the Oakland Raiders with the 10th pick.

Dan's Notes: I remember the hilarious old Vikings parodies created by the Twin Cities' KQRS radio station. One featured fake conversations between Nelson and Herschel Walker.

> BERNIE KOSAR VS. MIKE LYNN

On April 9, 1985, Vikings general manager Mike Lynn traded a first- and second-round pick to move up in the NFL draft, with plans to select University of Miami quarterback Bernie Kosar. However, Kosar had other ideas. Being from Ohio, he wanted to play for Cleveland. He conveniently neglected to get his draft eligibility paperwork to the league office in time, which made him ineligible for the regular draft. He could then be selected in the supplemental draft later that summer. Also conveniently, the Browns had traded to obtain the first overall pick in the supplemental draft. Kosar went to the Browns. It wasn't a total disaster for the Vikings, though. Because we couldn't pick Kosar, we selected defensive end—and future

hall-of-famer—Chris Doleman. The format of the supplemental draft later changed—but not before another college standout, Brian Bosworth (LB), pulled the same trick in 1987.

> COACH BURNS MELTS DOWN . . . AFTER A WIN:

In a 1989 season that saw the offense sputter—even with the addition of Herschel Walker (page 34)—Vikings offensive coordinator Bob Schnelker began to take some heat. According to the *Star Tribune's* Patrick Reusse, on November 5, someone passed out anti-Schnelker stickers before Minnesota's game versus the Los Angeles Rams at the Metrodome. During the game, Schnelker was booed. The Vikings offense scored 21 points on seven Rich Karlis field goals and won in overtime when linebacker Mike Merriweather blocked a punt that went out the back of the end zone for a safety. On his way off the field, Schnelker allegedly had beer poured on him. In the post-game press conference, head coach Jerry Burns declared, "As long as I'm in this [expletive] job, Schnelker will be the offensive coach." He went on an epic, profanity-laced tirade in support of his offensive coordinator. In more than four minutes of ranting, Burns dropped 18 F-bombs. He tried to leave the podium a few times, but every time he did, a quick-thinking reporter asked another question to keep him going. When he finally did leave the podium, he did so with one word, which rhymes with "suckers."

> THE ORIGINAL WHIZZINATOR:

In the fourth round of the 2003 draft, the Vikings selected running back Onterrio Smith from the University of Oregon.

Smith had originally played college football in Tennessee, but he was kicked off the team for marijuana use. He was suspended by the NFL for four games during the 2004 season after testing positive for marijuana in his system. On April 21, 2005, Smith was stopped by security at the Minneapolis-Saint Paul International Airport because something in his bag caught their attention. Upon further inspection, security officers found vials of a white powder and a prosthetic replica of male genitalia. Smith was taken to a back room, where he was questioned about the powder. He admitted that it was dried urine, and he explained that the prosthetic was a device called a Whizzinator, which was used to beat drug tests. The user would add water to the dried urine, fill the Whizzinator with the fake urine, and wear the Whizzinator to "urinate"—and avoid failing a drug test. Smith told airport police that the device was for his cousin, and he was not arrested. In June, Smith was suspended by the league for all of the 2005 season after a third violation of the NFL's substance abuse policy. The Vikings later released him, and he never played in the NFL again. The term "Whizzinator" remains a staple in the Minnesota sports fans' lexicon.

Dan's Notes: Smith's Whizzinator was auctioned off in 2009. It was purchased for $750 by Buster's Sports Bar & Grill in Mankato, Minnesota, as an attraction for Vikings fans.

CHAPTER 6
DISORDER IN DINKYTOWN

Ski-U-Mah. It's a phrase that all Minnesota Golden Gophers fans know. It's in the lyrics to the "Minnesota Rouser." The origin of the phrase has been attributed to former rugby captain John Adams. In 1884, he overheard Native American children yell, "Ski-yoo!" after winning a canoe race. He mistakenly thought it was their native word for "victory." In 2007, the Twin Cities' KARE 11 looked into the origin of the phrase and determined that it did not mean "victory." It may have been a celebratory exclamation, like "Yahoo!" Or it may have been used as encouragement, as in "Try harder!" If it's the latter, Adams' mistaken meaning of the call is comically ironic, especially when viewed through the lens of Minnesota sports heartbreak. As for our beloved NCAA Men's Division I sports teams, they've given us plenty to laugh—and cry—about.

GOPHERS MISS CHANCE TO HIRE LEGENDARY COACH WOODEN

 April 20, 1948   HEARTBREAK RATING:

> WHAT HAPPENED:

John Wooden is widely considered the greatest college basketball coach of all time. Before reaching that legendary status, he coached at Indiana State Teachers College from 1946 to 1948. After leading them to a second conference championship in 1948, Wooden became a candidate to coach the U of M men's basketball team. The University of California, Los Angeles (UCLA) was also pursuing Wooden. On April 20, 1948, he was officially announced as UCLA's new head coach. Those are the facts. Following is the story behind those facts.

Wooden preferred the Minnesota coaching job because his wife wished to stay in the Midwest. The U of M offered him the position but asked him to keep current head coach Dave MacMillan as an assistant. Wooden wanted to bring in his own assistants and didn't want to keep MacMillan. The U of M's athletic director, Frank McCormick, had to get permission to let MacMillan go and told Wooden that he would get back to him. Wooden waited for McCormick to call at the designated time, but the phone never rang. A blizzard had knocked down phone lines, which prevented McCormick from getting through. When McCormick finally reached Wooden, it was too late. The coach

John Wooden's Bruins won
the championship in 1971.

thought that the U of M had changed its mind, so he accepted the UCLA job instead.

> WHY IT HURT SO MUCH:

Wooden almost coached here; let that sink in. Missing out on one of basketball's greatest coaches is heartbreaking. If a snowstorm truly prevented it from happening, that's just piling on (pun intended). Our weather has been blamed, over the years, as a reason we can't attract the best players to our teams.

> THE AFTERMATH:

Wooden coached at UCLA for 27 seasons, and his teams won 10 championships—more than any other NCAA Division I men's basketball coach in history. Minnesota hired Osborne "Ozzie" Cowles, who coached the Gophers for 11 seasons and compiled a respectable 147–93 record. MacMillan was not kept on as an assistant coach but was given another job at the university.

> DAN'S NOTES:

The blizzard in this story may be more legend than fact. In Wooden's book, *A Game Plan for Life*, he said the missed call from the U of M was to come on a Sunday (April 18, 1948). In looking through the Minneapolis weather data for that weekend, the temperature ranged between 39 and 78 degrees, with no precipitation. Sid Hartman suggested in a 2010 article that the blizzard occurred in South Dakota, but I found similar weather data there and no mention of a blizzard.

GOPHERS GET INTO "BRAWL AT THE BARN" WITH OHIO STATE

 January 25, 1972   HEARTBREAK RATING:

> WHAT HAPPENED:

On April 5, 1971, the U of M named Bill Musselman the new men's basketball coach. Musselman was known for his intense coaching style and a focus on defense. That fall, our team went 6–3 in the nonconference schedule and started 4–0 in the Big Ten Conference, earning a rank of 16th in the country. That set up a showdown at Williams Arena (also known as "the Barn") with the sixth-ranked Ohio State Buckeyes in a battle for first place in the Big Ten. Reportedly, some 17,775 fans attended and were whipped into a frenzy by Minnesota's Harlem-Globetrotters-esque pregame warmups.

At halftime, tempers flared on the way to the locker room, and the teams exchanged words. Tensions remained high throughout the second half. With 36 seconds left in the game, Ohio State led, 50–44. Buckeyes center Luke Witte was fouled by Minnesota's Clyde Taylor. Witte ended up on the ground; Taylor helped him up—and then kneed him in the groin. The benches cleared. Fans stormed the court, and a brawl began. The Gophers' Ron Behagen reportedly came off the bench to stomp on Witte's head and had to be pulled away. Minnesota's Dave Winfield also came off the bench and, according to *The*

Minneapolis Star, "got in some real punches" on Ohio State forward Mark Minor. Ohio State forward Mark Wagar was hit by a fan. When order was restored, Gophers athletic director Paul Giel announced that the game was over. Ohio State won.

WHY IT HURT SO MUCH:

It's been called one of the worst moments in Minnesota sports history and is undoubtedly one of the most shameful. Not only did our players lose their composure in a big moment, they— and some of our fans—acted with shocking violence. One observer (who was a child at the time) said in an interview with KFAN's Scott Korzenowski that it was the first time he'd seen order break down, and he felt sick to his stomach.

> THE AFTERMATH:

Ohio State's coach felt the incident began with the Gophers' pregame warmup, which he didn't find appropriate. Musselman believed the incident started at halftime, when Witte was said to have elbowed Gophers guard Bob Nix in the head. For Taylor's part, he said that he attacked Witte because the center had spit on him.

Minor was treated for cuts and bruises. Witte was hospitalized overnight. On January 28, the Big Ten suspended Behagen and Taylor for the rest of the season but ruled that Minnesota would be allowed to continue the pregame routine. The Gophers did not play Ohio State again that season, but we did win the Big Ten title. We lost our first game in the NCAA tournament to Florida State, 70–56.

GOPHERS PUNISHED FOR MUSSELMAN-ERA VIOLATIONS

 March 9, 1976 HEARTBREAK RATING: ♥♥♥♡♡

> WHAT HAPPENED:

In Bill Musselman's first year as head coach (page 189), the Minnesota Golden Gophers appeared in the 1972 College Basketball NCAA Tournament. Three years later, on July 23, 1975, the U of M received a letter from the NCAA accusing the basketball program of an estimated 100 violations, which included players selling game tickets for more than face value and players receiving cash and other freebies that were considered "excessive aid" from boosters and from Musselman. Five days later, Musselman claimed that he didn't feel supported by the U of M and took a job coaching the American Basketball Association's San Diego Sails.

On December 18, the NCAA asked the university to declare three players—Mychal Thompson, Phil "Flip" Saunders, and Dave Winey—ineligible. The U of M was told that if they did so, the university's penalties would be greatly lessened. On January 12, 1976, Thompson and Saunders were declared ineligible. Thompson fought his suspension with an attorney, and the matter still wasn't resolved on March 9, when the NCAA released its report on the violations. The NCAA handed down sanctions against the team, including scholarship reductions and no postseason tournaments or nationally televised games for two years, as well as three years of probation. In addition, our 1972 tournament appearance was vacated—or erased from the records.

> WHY IT HURT SO MUCH:

The Gophers didn't have a storied postseason history. In fact, 1972 was our first ever appearance in the NCAA tournament. Having said that, fans felt that it could be the beginning of something big. It was disheartening to have it all taken away. Plus, Musselman left unpunished—with the university and his players holding the bag.

> THE AFTERMATH:

A U of M hearing determined on May 5 that "there was not a sufficient basis to declare these students ineligible." The NCAA responded by putting the entire men's athletic department on probation, which excluded all teams from postseason play. After a lengthy appeals process, the NCAA's punishment went into effect on August 4, 1977. On October 24, with the football team in the midst of a successful season, the U of M declared Thompson and Winey ineligible. (Saunders was no longer on the team.) The NCAA lifted the probation off the rest of the men's teams on November 7. Thompson sat out the first six games of the 1977–1978 season; Winey missed the first two games. Because of the battle, the NCAA extended probation on the men's basketball program until October 1978. The team finished the 1977–1978 season with a 17–10 record, but we were ineligible for postseason play because of the extension.

MINNESOTA GOPHERS FOOT-BALL MOVES TO METRODOME

 April 16, 1982

HEARTBREAK RATING:

> WHAT HAPPENED:

On October 14, 1924, our Minnesota Golden Gophers football team played their first game at Memorial Stadium. The stadium was named for the U of M students and staff who had served in World War I. While calling the stadium home, the Gophers won six national championships and 10 Big Ten championships, enjoyed six unbeaten seasons, and even had a Heisman Trophy winner (Bruce Smith, 1941). But by the early 1980s, Memorial Stadium was old—and starting to show it. It required an estimated $3 million to $10.5 million to maintain and renovate.

At the time, the Metropolitan Sports Facilities Commission (MSFC) was building a new domed stadium for the Minnesota Twins and Vikings. The U of M began to consider whether the Gophers should play there too. University officials felt that moving would help recruiting, increase season-ticket sales, and boost attendance. On November 21, 1981, we lost our final game at Memorial Stadium to the Wisconsin Badgers, 26–21.

On April 16, 1982, the U of M's board of regents voted to move the football team to the new Metrodome beginning with the 1982 season. The contract stipulated that the university would

The Hubert H. Humphrey Metrodome was home to the Gophers, Twins, and Vikings.

receive free rent and all gate receipts (less 10% for the MSFC), plus 35% of concession profits. The lease was for 30 years, but the university could withdraw from the contract at any time during the first three years. In that first season at the Dome, the Gophers went 3–8, but the average attendance of 58,898 was significantly greater than 1981's average of 43,035.

Three years later, on December 14, 1984, head coach Lou Holtz (page 198) gave an impassioned speech (that resembled a pre-game pep talk) in favor of staying at the Dome. The board of regents voted to lock into the lease for the remaining 27 years.

> WHY IT HURT SO MUCH:

Moving football indoors felt different. Fans missed the autumn air, the tailgating, and the community that went with outdoor football—on campus. Fans also yearned for the days when the Gophers were a dominant force. Memorial Stadium was the backdrop for those memories, making it hard to let go.

> THE AFTERMATH:

In the years that followed, attendance averages slipped down again. Playing away from campus became a hindrance to recruiting, according to some. Plus, the U of M missed out on revenue from parking and from selling suites. Memorial Stadium was demolished in 1992. Bricks from the stadium were sold as souvenirs for $10. Some of the bricks were used in building the entrance to the Mariucci Hockey Arena. In 2006, the state legislature approved funding for a $248 million on-campus football stadium, which would become TCF Bank Stadium.

MINNESOTA GOPHERS LOSE BY 71 POINTS TO NEBRASKA

 September 17, 1983   HEARTBREAK RATING:

> WHAT HAPPENED:

The Minnesota Golden Gophers won the opening game of the 1983 football season against Rice University, 21–17. The next week, on September 17, we hosted the Nebraska Cornhuskers, the number-one team in the country. The Cornhuskers were an offensive juggernaut, and Minnesota head coach Joe Salem knew it would be a difficult test.

If Salem thought the Metrodome's crowd noise would help us, Nebraska quickly put an end to that notion. They only needed a few minutes to begin the onslaught, scoring on a Mark Schellen 27-yard run. Nebraska missed the extra point, but that would be the only thing to go wrong for the Cornhuskers. They scored twice more in the quarter, both on long touchdown passes from Turner Gill to Irving Fryar—and they added a two-point conversion from Gill to Fryar to take a 21–0 lead. The Gophers got on the scoreboard at the beginning of the second quarter with a David Puk one-yard touchdown plunge. Nebraska added three more touchdowns on runs from Fryar (41 yards), Jeff Smith (12 yards), and Mike Rozier (7 yards). Minnesota's Jim Gallery kicked a field goal in the midst of that stampede. The halftime score favored Nebraska, 42–10.

The third quarter was more of the same, with three touchdown runs for Nebraska, by Gill (12 yards) and Rozier (1 yard and 71 yards). The Gophers mixed in another field goal.

The Cornhuskers' backup quarterback Craig Sundberg took over in the fourth. He added a 51-yard touchdown pass to Smith, and he ran for two touchdowns (44 yards and 1 yard).

When all was said and done, the Gophers lost, 84–13. Nebraska amassed 790 yards of total offense, including 595 yards rushing (196 yards by Rozier). The Cornhuskers only completed five passes but racked up 195 yards through the air.

> WHY IT HURT SO MUCH:

This wasn't heartbreaking; it was embarrassing. It was officially the worst loss in Gophers football history: the most points ever given up and the widest margin of defeat. After the game, Nebraska head coach Tom Osborne apologized for scoring so many points. He said they weren't trying to run up the score.

> THE AFTERMATH:

Two weeks later, the Gophers got thumped again, this time by the eighth-ranked Ohio State Buckeyes, 69–18. After losing six games in a row, Salem resigned on October 25, but he agreed to coach the Gophers until the end of the season. He finished 1983 with a 1–10 record (0–9 in the conference), good enough for last place in the Big 10—for the second year in a row. Lou Holtz was hired in December 1983 as Minnesota's new college football head coach (page 198).

LOU HOLTZ LEAVES GOPHERS TO COACH AT NOTRE DAME

 November 27, 1985   HEARTBREAK RATING:

> WHAT HAPPENED:

After the 1983 football season, the Minnesota Golden Gophers were in search of a new head coach. A name that surfaced was Lou Holtz, the head coach at the University of Arkansas. In seven seasons there, Holtz had led Arkansas to a 60–21–2 record and six postseason bowl appearances. On December 18, he resigned from Arkansas. When Holtz was contacted about the Minnesota job, he initially declined because he didn't like cold weather. But he quickly warmed to the idea and was named our head coach on December 22.

In Holtz's first season, the Gophers improved from 1–10 to 4–7. In his second season, the Gophers went 6–5 and played in our first bowl game since the 1977 season. Meanwhile, rumors swirled that Notre Dame was going to fire their head coach and that Holtz was interested in the job. Holtz said, "There isn't a job in the country that I'd leave Minnesota for with the possible exception of Notre Dame." On November 26, the Notre Dame job opened, and it was offered to Holtz. He still had three years left on his Minnesota contract, but that contract included a stipulation that would allow him to leave if a certain team came calling. According to Holtz, "the only stipulation we did put in was if Notre Dame ever did contact me, I would feel free to go." On November 27, Holtz was introduced as the head coach of the Notre Dame Fighting Irish football team.

> WHY IT HURT SO MUCH:

After nearly two decades of futility, it was beginning to look like our football program was finally on its way to prominence again. The fact that Holtz included a stipulation about one specific team—and that one team actually did come and get him—is just our luck. This introduced the term "Notre Dame Clause" into the Minnesota sports lexicon, and hearing it still makes us shake our heads in frustration.

> THE AFTERMATH:

On December 5, Holtz's assistant John Gutekunst became the Gophers head football coach. In the Independence Bowl, he coached us to victory over Clemson, 20–13. Gutekunst coached the Gophers for six full seasons but never won more than six games in a season. Holtz coached at Notre Dame for 11 seasons and compiled a record of 100–30–2. He appeared in nine consecutive bowl games and won a national championship in 1988. In 1991, there were rumors that the Minnesota Vikings wanted to hire him, but they chose Denny Green instead. Holtz resigned from Notre Dame on November 19, 1996. Rumors again suggested that the Vikings would hire him, but the Vikings kept Green. Holtz went on to coach the University of South Carolina for six seasons and led them to two bowl appearances.

MINNESOTA GOPHERS FALL ONE GAME SHORT OF FINAL FOUR

 March 25, 1990   HEARTBREAK RATING:

> WHAT HAPPENED:

The 1989–1990 roster of the Minnesota Golden Gophers men's basketball team included Walter Bond, Willie Burton, Richard Coffey, Kevin Lynch, Melvin Newbern, and Jim Shikenjanski. Led by head coach Clem Haskins, the team finished with a 23–9 record and earned a sixth seed in the 1990 NCAA Division I Men's Basketball Tournament. In the opening round, we squeaked by Texas-El Paso, 64–61, in overtime. Two days later, we defeated Northern Iowa (who had upset the third-seeded Missouri Tigers), 81–78, and advanced to the Sweet 16 for the second year in a row. Most experts expected our run to end there because we faced Syracuse, a second seed in the tournament and the sixth-ranked team in the country. But we played one of our best games of the season and made nearly 80% of our shots in the second half. The Gophers scored a momentous victory and a major upset, 82–75.

Just one game from the Final Four, Minnesota matched up against the Georgia Tech Yellow Jackets in the Elite Eight. A fourth seed, Georgia Tech was not expected to be as tough as Syracuse; our team could certainly beat them. The Yellow Jackets were led by Dennis Scott, Brian Oliver, and freshman

Willie Burton broke his nose before the 1989 NCAA tournament and had to wear a protective mask.

point guard Kenny Anderson. Minnesota built a 12-point lead in the first half, but Georgia Tech rallied to cut our lead to 49–47 at halftime. The second half was a seesaw affair. The Gophers trailed by five points in the game's final seconds, but Burton hit a three-pointer to bring the score to 93–91. With six seconds on the clock, the Gophers fouled Anderson. He missed his free throw, and Minnesota had a chance. We got the ball down the court in a hurry, and Lynch threw up a shot at the buzzer, but he missed.

Georgia Tech's Scott led all scorers with 40 points; Anderson added 30. Burton paced Minnesota with 35 points. After the game, there was some criticism of the referees because Georgia Tech shot 35 free throws, while the Gophers were only sent to the line 11 times.

> WHY IT HURT SO MUCH:

This was the furthest a Minnesota team had ever gotten, and the 23 regular-season wins tied for second-most in team history. However, this seemed like the end of the run. Burton, Coffey, Newbern, and Shikenjanski were all seniors. We missed our chance; the team would have to rebuild.

> THE AFTERMATH:

Burton was picked ninth overall in the NBA draft by the Miami Heat. He played eight seasons in the NBA. Coffey and Newbern each spent a year in the NBA. The following season, the Gophers won just 12 games. Lynch played in the NBA for two seasons, and Bond was in the NBA for four.

GOPHERS BLOW A 21-POINT LEAD IN THE FOURTH QUARTER

 October 10, 2003   HEARTBREAK RATING:

WHAT HAPPENED:

Glen Mason was in his seventh season as the Minnesota Gophers head football coach in 2003. The Gophers started 6–0, our best record since 1960 (when our team won the national championship). On October 10, the 17th-ranked Gophers hosted the 20th-ranked Michigan Wolverines at the Metrodome. It was such a big game that it was televised on ESPN. However, the Gophers had lost 14 straight games to the Wolverines.

Behind four rushing touchdowns, including two by running back Laurence Maroney, Minnesota powered to a 28–7 lead entering the fourth quarter. That was when something changed. The Gophers, who had held Michigan's offense at bay, suddenly couldn't figure them out. Michigan scored 26 seconds into the fourth quarter on a 10-yard touchdown pass. A few plays later, quarterback Asad Abdul-Khaliq threw an interception that was returned for a touchdown—and suddenly the score was 28–21. On our next possession Abdul-Khaliq answered for Minnesota with a 52-yard touchdown run through the middle of Michigan's defense. The Wolverines then connected on a 52-yard touchdown pass to star receiver Braylon Edwards, bringing Michigan to within seven points again. With less than six minutes to go, a 10-yard touchdown run for the Wolverines tied the game at 35. Then, in the final minutes, they put together a methodical drive that ate up most of the clock. Kicker Garrett Rivas booted a 33-yard game-winning field goal for Michigan with 47 seconds to go. The Gophers lost, 38–35.

> WHY IT HURT SO MUCH:

If we had won this game, we could've been ranked in the top 10. Instead, we choked in front of 62,374 fans at the Dome and a national TV audience. The Gophers gave up 31 points in that infamous fourth quarter and effectively blew our chance at playing in the Rose Bowl for the first time since 1962.

> THE AFTERMATH:

The Gophers lost two more games and played in the Sun Bowl, where we beat Oregon, 31–30. Michigan fell in the Rose Bowl to the University of Southern California. We lost to Michigan again in 2004. But in 2005, we upset the 21st-ranked Wolverines at the Big House in Ann Arbor on a last-second field goal.

> DAN'S NOTES:

I was at the game in 2003, sitting right behind the Michigan bench. When we were up by 21 points, I screamed at their team to "Bring out the jug!" (The Little Brown Jug is a trophy that the Michigan-Minnesota winner takes home each year.) But I'll never forget that fourth quarter. Michigan seemingly ran the same screen pass over and over, and we couldn't stop it. Fifteen minutes later, I was sick to my stomach, with my head in my hands, trying to process what I had just witnessed.

Laurence Maroney was drafted by New England in the first round of the 2006 NFL Draft.

HOLY CROSS UPSETS GOPHERS IN THE NCAA TOURNAMENT

 March 24, 2006 HEARTBREAK RATING:

 WHAT HAPPENED:

In 2006, the Minnesota Gophers men's hockey team looked ready to win a third national championship in five seasons. In the first round of the NCAA Division I Men's Ice Hockey Tournament, the first-seeded Gophers faced a fourth-seeded team, the Holy Cross Crusaders. At the time, fourth seeds were 0–15 in the tournament format that included 16 teams.

In the first period, the Gophers looked lethargic and the game was scoreless. In the second, the Crusaders scored at the 8:49 mark. The Gophers' Mike Howe answered five minutes later. But 30 seconds after that, the Crusaders took the lead again on a power play goal. Minnesota tied it back up when Phil Kessel scored with about four minutes left in the period. Minnesota's Alex Goligoski gave us our first lead in the third period, but Holy Cross responded by tying the game. Regulation ended with the score knotted, 3–3.

Just 53 seconds into the extra period, the Crusaders' Tyler MacGregor attempted a pass to a teammate who was heading toward the net. Minnesota goalkeeper Kellen Briggs slid to his left to follow the puck. But the pass hit a Gopher's skate and bounced back to MacGregor. He easily put the puck into the open side of the net, shocking the college hockey world and giving Holy Cross their first ever NCAA tournament victory. The Gophers had seven power play chances in the game and didn't score on any of them.

> WHY IT HURT SO MUCH:

The Gophers were ranked third in the country (and were ranked first for most of the season). Holy Cross had been a Division I hockey team for just eight years, and this was only their second NCAA tournament appearance. It was considered one of the biggest upsets in the history of the tournament.

> THE AFTERMATH:

Holy Cross lost to North Dakota, 5–2, in the next round. The Gophers returned to the NCAA tournament seven times over the next 14 years and advanced to the Frozen Four in 2012 and 2014 but did not win a championship.

> DAN'S NOTES:

During the 2002 national championship game, the Gophers were down, 3–2, late in the third period. When our team tied the game, I was on my way to a restaurant and heard it on the radio. At the restaurant, I watched on TV and saw the Gophers score what I thought was the winning goal. I stood up and cheered. Everyone else in the restaurant just stared at me; it was a replay of the game-tying goal. When the Gophers did score the game-winner in overtime, everyone jokingly assured me that it was now okay to stand up and cheer.

MINNESOTA GOPHERS BLOW 31-POINT LEAD IN BOWL GAME

 December 29, 2006   HEARTBREAK RATING:

 WHAT HAPPENED:

In the 35 seasons that followed the Minnesota Golden Gophers' last Rose Bowl appearance, our football team qualified for a total of three bowl games: the Hall of Fame Classic (1977), the Independence Bowl (1985), and the Liberty Bowl (1986). In December 1996, Glen Mason was hired as the team's head coach. In his first nine seasons, he led the Gophers to six bowl games. However, his overall record was a mediocre 58–50, and his conference record was 29-43.

In 2006, Mason's Gophers started 2–5. Then, on October 21, we narrowly defeated North Dakota State University, 10–9. The following week, Minnesota lost to top-ranked Ohio State University, 44–0. We finished the season with three straight wins, which made us eligible for a bowl game with a record of 6–6. The Gophers were invited to the Insight Bowl in Tempe, Arizona, to play the Texas Tech Red Raiders.

We dominated the first half, rolling to a 35–7 lead. A Minnesota field goal midway through the third quarter made it 38–7. The Red Raiders responded by scoring four unanswered touchdowns, bringing the score to 38–35 with less than three minutes to go. Texas Tech attempted an onside kick that went out of bounds, which gave Minnesota the ball at midfield with 2:20 on the clock. Our team couldn't manage a first down and was forced to punt. Texas Tech quickly moved the ball into Minnesota territory, and kicker Alex Trlica hit a career-long 52-yard field goal to send the game into overtime. The Gophers put a field goal on the board, but Texas Tech won the game with a three-yard touchdown run, completing the largest comeback victory in Division I-A bowl history.

> WHY IT HURT SO MUCH:

Mason's offense was historic: He had two running backs rush for more than 1,000 yards in two consecutive seasons. His defense, however, was infamously known for big letdowns (page 203). This game was the worst of them. It was hard, even embarrassing, to watch.

> THE AFTERMATH:

Even before this night, many fans had already turned on the coach, chanting "Fire Mason!" at home games. Two days after the Insight Bowl, Mason was let go. On January 16, 2007, Tim Brewster was hired as the new coach. He went 15–30 before getting canned during his fourth season. Mason went on to become an analyst for the Big Ten Network.

> DAN'S NOTES:

I am now ashamed to admit that I brought a sign to Gophers games that said "Fire Mason!" My mother always used to say to me, "Be careful what you wish for."

MINNESOTA GOPHERS HOCKEY TEAM LEAVES THE WCHA

 March 21, 2011   HEARTBREAK RATING:

> WHAT HAPPENED:

The Midwest Collegiate Hockey League was formed on November 28, 1951. Its original teams were Colorado College, Denver, Michigan, Michigan State, Michigan Tech, Minnesota, and North Dakota. On March 8, 1959, six of the teams formed a new conference called the Western Collegiate Hockey Conference (WCHA). The seventh team, Michigan, would eventually join, as well. Over the years, the league's membership expanded and changed, but the Gophers remained.

In September 2010, Penn State University announced that they would add hockey as a varsity sport in 2012. It would make them the sixth Big Ten school with a hockey program, and Big Ten rules stipulated that there must be six teams "before they [could] play for a conference championship." On March 21, 2011, the Big Ten announced that it would form its own hockey conference to begin play in 2013. Member teams included Michigan, Michigan State, Minnesota, Ohio State, Penn State, and Wisconsin. This meant that the Gophers would leave the WCHA after the 2012–2013 season. (The decision only affected the men's team. There still weren't enough women's hockey teams in the Big Ten.)

WHY IT HURT SO MUCH:

The traditional rivalries that our hockey team shared with North Dakota and the other Minnesota teams, especially Duluth, were gone. Even though the teams could still play against each other in nonconference matchups, it wasn't the same. Fans would never get as excited for Penn State coming to town as they did for a WCHA game against North Dakota.

> THE AFTERMATH:

Colorado College, Denver, North Dakota, Nebraska-Omaha, Duluth, and Saint Cloud also left the WCHA and formed the National Collegiate Hockey Conference. The WCHA added Alaska-Fairbanks, Bowling Green, Ferris State, Lake Superior State, and Northern Michigan. The Gophers finished fifth in the 2013–2014 Big Ten standings.

> DAN'S NOTES:

The biggest casualty in all of this has been attendance. There was a clear drop in hockey attendance after the move to the Big Ten Conference. There has also been a decrease in season ticket sales. Before the conference realignment, the U of M's Mariucci Arena was often packed and rocking, especially when North Dakota or one of the other Minnesota teams was in town. In addition, the WCHA conference tournament used to be a hot ticket. The 2013 WCHA Men's Ice Hockey Tournament Finals averaged 18,095 fans per game. The 2019 Big Ten Men's Ice Hockey Tournament Finals averaged 5,138.

North Dakota was one
of the Gophers' biggest
rivals in the WCHA.

QUICK HITS: GOPHER GAFFS

> NCAA INVESTIGATIONS FIND MANY VIOLATIONS:

On May 30, 1986, U of M athletic director Paul Giel announced that the NCAA would investigate our basketball team. After an 18-month investigation, with cooperation from the university, the NCAA cited 40 violations, including the selling of game tickets by players for financial gain. On March 7, 1988, the NCAA placed our men's basketball team on probation for two years. In cooperating with the NCAA, the U of M spent $300,000 on investigative attorneys. A month later, Luther Darville, an administrator for the university's Office of Minority and Special Student Affairs, was investigated for misappropriating nearly $200,000 of university funds for himself and giving payments to students, including nine football players. Darville reportedly believed that he was acting under orders from Frank Wilderson, Jr., the U of M's vice president for student affairs. Darville was fired and indicted on charges of theft. He fled to the Bahamas. Interim university president Richard Sauer fired Giel on July 5 and removed Wilderson from overseeing athletics. (Wilderson resigned in December.) Darville was extradited from the Bahamas in August 1989. Three months later, he was found guilty and sentenced to 18 months in prison. In March 1990, the U of M's investigative attorneys reported additional violations in the tennis and wrestling programs. That cost the university another estimated $300,000 in legal fees. In December 1990, the NCAA began another investigation. Three months later, they found us guilty of 17 rules violations. As a result, most notably, the entire men's athletic department was put on probation for two years.

> TRICK SHOT OUSTS GOPHERS FROM TOURNEY:

On March 23, 1996, in the first round of the NCAA tournament, the third-seeded Gophers beat the Providence Friars, 5–1. Two days later, the Gophers faced the second-seeded Michigan Wolverines for a chance to advance to the Frozen Four. The Gophers dominated from the start and gained a 2–1 lead. However, momentum changed in the second period because of a unique goal. Michigan's Mike Legg had the puck behind the Gophers' net. In one swift motion, Legg used the blade of his stick to lift the puck, like a pizza on a tray. He then reached his stick around and tucked the puck into the upper corner of the net, over the left shoulder of our goalkeeper, Steve DeBus. The goal tied the score, and Legg's goal gave Michigan a spark that changed the game. Michigan eventually won, 4–3. Gophers coach Doug Woog later said, "We had them. You know when you have somebody on the ropes."

Michigan beat Boston University and Colorado College to win the national championship. Legg's stick was sent to the Hockey Hall of Fame, and his play won "Goal of the Year" from *Inside Hockey* magazine. It was also nominated for an ESPN ESPY Award. Some NHL players have since attempted Legg's trick shot. Andrei Svechnikov of the Carolina Hurricanes scored twice with it in 2019. The NHL ruled that, as long as the stick is kept below the shoulders, it is a legal play.

CHAPTER 7
DISTRESSED OF THE REST

Someone once suggested an event for our Minnesota Sports Disappointment Calendar about a Minnesota Olympian who failed to win a gold medal. That sparked a *WHEN-ESOTA?* debate about whether or not individual sports and athletes should be calendar-eligible. The outcome of that discussion was that, yes, individual sports are considered—but the event has to be particularly calamitous. Missing out on a gold medal is not calendar-worthy unless the loss occurs in some spectacular fashion. This chapter is for individual sports that made the calendar, as well as some events that didn't fit perfectly into the other chapters. It's not a hodgepodge but rather a "hotdish," if you will, of Minnesota sports heartbreaks.

PROFESSIONAL GOLFERS RIP NEW MINNESOTA COURSE

 June 19, 1970   HEARTBREAK RATING:

> WHAT HAPPENED:

In 1962, Hazeltine National Golf Club opened for play on a 1,400-acre site in Chaska, Minnesota, near Lake Hazeltine. In 1966, the course hosted the U.S. Women's Open, its first national championship tournament. On January 28, 1967, the United States Golf Association (USGA) announced that the 1970 U.S. Open would be held at Hazeltine, June 18–21.

A month before the tournament, legendary golfer Jack Nicklaus played a practice round at Hazeltine and wrote about it in *Sports Illustrated*. According to his article, he "frequently felt lost," and he added, "at Hazeltine, everything is blind." In response, course architect Robert Trent Jones fired back that Nicklaus was the one who was blind.

On Day 1 of the tournament, 40-mile-per-hour winds resulted in abnormally high scores. On Day 2, the weather was much improved. A brash golfer from Michigan named Dave Hill shot a 69 and moved into second place. He truly stole the spotlight with his post-round comments. Hill was upset with the course and was upset that so many big-name players were struggling. A reporter asked him how he liked the golf course. Hill didn't hold back: "If I had to play this course every day for fun, I'd find another game. . . . How did I find the golf course? I've been trying to find it ever since I came to Minneapolis. . . . Just because you cut the grass and put up flags doesn't mean you have a golf course. . . . What does it lack? Eighty acres of corn and a few cows. . . . They ruined a good farm by building this golf course on it. . . . My two kids could lay out a better course than that. . . . The man who designed this course had the blueprints upside down."

> WHY IT HURT SO MUCH:

Minnesotans are proud of our heritage and culture. When we host big events, we want to showcase our state and let the rest of the world know what Minnesota has to offer. Our sports fans—and non-fans—took Hill's comments personally. To us, he wasn't attacking a golf course; he was attacking our state. It's safe to say that our collective feelings were hurt.

> THE AFTERMATH:

The next day, Hill was fined $150 by the Professional Golfers' Association of America. (He wasn't the only critical player, just the most vocal about it.) He ultimately lost to Tony Jacklin by seven strokes. After the tournament, Hazeltine made changes to the course, based on players' suggestions. In 1991, the U.S. Open returned to Hazeltine. The summer before, Hill came back to play Hazeltine with Rees Jones, son of Robert Trent Jones, as a promotional event to kick off ticket sales. After shooting a par 72, Hill praised the course.

THE MINNESOTA KICKS LOSE THE SOCCER BOWL

 August 28,1976   HEARTBREAK RATING:

> WHAT HAPPENED:

With an increase in the popularity of soccer in the 1970s, a group of 10 investors announced on November 25, 1975, that Minnesota would get its first professional soccer team. The group purchased the Denver Dynamos of the North American Soccer League (NASL) and brought the team to Minnesota. A contest was held to name the team, and more than 3,500 entries were received. The team was officially named the Minnesota Kicks on January 28, 1976.

Our Kicks played their first match on April 24 and lost to the Earthquakes in San Jose, 4–2. A few weeks later, on May 9, the Kicks got revenge, beating the Earthquakes, 4–1, in our home opener. Nevertheless, the Kicks lost nine of the first 15 matches. But then our team turned the season around. We won nine of our last 10 and finished first in the Western Division.

In the first playoff match, on August 21, Kicks goalkeeper Geoff Barnett earned his eighth shutout of the season as the Kicks beat the Seattle Sounders, 3–0. Four days later, in front of a crowd of 49,572 fans, the Kicks beat San Jose, 3–1, to advance to the NASL Championship. In all the excitement, fans rushed the field. The sprinklers were turned on to clear away the fans, but those present continued to dance in the water.

The NASL Championship, known as the Soccer Bowl, was held at the Kingdome in Seattle on August 28. The Kicks were favored over the Toronto Metros, who had been underdogs in each of their playoff games but were riding a seven-game winning streak. In the game, the Kicks had some scoring chances but couldn't find the back of the net. The Kicks' dream season came to a heartbreaking close as our team lost, 3–0. The Kicks had not been shut out all season until the Soccer Bowl.

> WHY IT HURT SO MUCH:

The Minnesota Twins had lost a World Series (page 104) and the Minnesota Vikings had lost three Super Bowls (pages 38–45). This added a third local team that missed out on a championship. Our state was getting a reputation for not being able to win the big game; Steve Berg from the *Star Tribune* called it the "Minnesota Syndrome."

> THE AFTERMATH:

It was the first and the last time the Kicks played in the Soccer Bowl. We qualified for the playoffs in each of our six seasons in the NASL, and we finished first in the Western Division four years in a row. Despite the team's popularity and success, the Kicks lost money. The team folded in December 1981 (page 227), and our players were sent to other teams via a dispersal draft.

METROPOLITAN STADIUM GETS DEMOLISHED

 January 28, 1985   HEARTBREAK RATING: 💜💜💜💜💜

WHAT HAPPENED:

On June 16, 1953, the Twin Cities were approved by MLB for a future baseball team. The team would need a stadium, so farmland in Bloomington was purchased. The groundbreaking for the stadium was held on June 20, 1955, and the stadium was built in less than a year. The first game was played on April 24, 1956. A crowd of 18,366 watched minor-league baseball's Minneapolis Millers lose to the Wichita Braves, 5–4. The site was officially named Metropolitan Stadium (the Met) on July 19.

On October 26, 1960, Washington Senators owner Calvin Griffith announced that his team would move to Minnesota. The team was renamed the Minnesota Twins, and our MLB club played its first home game on April 21, 1961; we lost, 5–3, to the new expansion Washington Senators. The Minnesota Vikings arrived in 1961. On September 17, in our first NFL game, we upset the Chicago Bears, 37–13.

On September 30, 1981, the Twins played a final game at the Met and lost to the Kansas City Royals, 5–2. On December 20, the Vikings closed out the stadium with a 10–6 loss to the Kansas City Chiefs (page 150). Met Stadium was abandoned, left unattended, and was even vandalized. On January 28, 1985, demolition began. About 350 people were on hand to witness the beginning of the demolition, including former players Harmon Killebrew (Twins), Mick Tingelhoff (Vikings), and Bill Brown (Vikings).

> WHY IT HURT SO MUCH:

Fans at the Met would tailgate before and after games—and were sometimes joined by players. It was relationship-building. A connectedness. A community. This was where Minnesota kids went to their first ball games. Those memories stir up thoughts of happy times. When we lost the Met, it hurt.

> THE AFTERMATH:

The Twins, Vikings, and Gophers football team all moved to the Hubert H. Humphrey Metrodome in 1982. Many fans felt that the indoor environment wasn't as lively for watching sports. Julian Empson Loscalzo, spokesperson for the Save the Met Committee, said the Dome was "a sterile, antiseptic, cold place." The Mall of America now stands where the Met once did. A commemorative home plate sits in the mall where Met Stadium's home plate once was. There is also a seat that commemorates where Killebrew's longest home run landed.

> DAN'S NOTES:

More than 25,000 fans saw The Beatles perform at the Met on August 21, 1965. On August 1, 1978, nearly 65,000 came to see The Eagles, the Steve Miller Band, and Pablo Cruise. That was the biggest crowd for any event in the stadium's history.

THE METRODOME'S ROOF COLLAPSES . . . FIVE TIMES

 1981–2014   HEARTBREAK RATING:

> NOVEMBER 18, 1981:

On October 2, 1981, the Hubert H. Humphrey Metrodome's ceiling was raised for the first time. The following month, on November 18, a snowstorm dropped 10.2 inches of snow. The weight of that snow caused the Dome's roof to partially collapse, making it look flat. Workers re-inflated it throughout the night. The next evening, however, as workers removed snow from the roof, they heard a *pop*. One of the roof's panels on the north side of the stadium had torn. Over the next hour, the Metrodome roof slowly collapsed.

> DECEMBER 30, 1982:

Workers were clearing snow from the roof. They accidentally caused a small avalanche of snow to fall off. This lessened the pressure, causing the roof to rise slightly. As it rose, it hit a metal bucket that was suspended over the Dome by a crane, creating a tear in the Teflon. The roof collapsed.

> APRIL 14, 1983:

A few months later, yet another unexpected snowstorm brought down the roof. That day, 13.6 inches of snow fell on the Twin Cities. At 11:30 p.m., falling ice and snow led to a 38-foot tear in the roof; workers deflated the Dome as a precautionary measure. Repairs were made just in time for baseball to be played the following night.

> APRIL 26, 1986:

It wasn't snow that did in the roof in 1986. The roof was affected by a 60- to 80-mile-per-hour gust of wind. In the eighth inning of a game between the Minnesota Twins and California Angels, the violent wind against the roof caused pressure inside the Dome to drop. As lights and speakers swayed, spectators were asked to wait in the concourse area. Electronic fans were turned on to help stabilize the pressure. After a nine-minute delay, the game resumed. The Angels scored six runs in the top of the ninth inning and won the game, 7–6.

> DECEMBER 12, 2010:

In 2010, the Metrodome roof tore and deflated beneath as much as 24 inches of snow. A game between the Minnesota Vikings and New York Giants had to be played at Ford Field in Detroit, Michigan. The following week, the Vikings hosted the Chicago Bears at the U of M's TCF Bank Stadium. We lost both games by a combined score of 61–17.

> THE AFTERMATH:

In 2012, the Minnesota Legislature approved funding for a new stadium to be built. Our Vikings played their last game at the Metrodome on December 29, 2013. We beat the Detroit Lions, 14–13. On January 18, 2014, the Metrodome roof was deflated for the final time, signifying the beginning of its demolition.

QUICK HITS: MORE MAYHEM

> HOWARD COSELL LOSES HIS TOUPEE:

Scott LeDoux was a professional boxer born in Crosby, Minnesota. In college, he played football for the University of Minnesota Duluth, where he was also introduced to boxing. Nicknamed "The Fighting Frenchman," LeDoux made his professional debut on February 4, 1974, when he knocked out Arthur Pullins in four rounds at the Minneapolis Convention Center. In LeDoux's nine-year professional career, he compiled a 33–13–4 record with 22 knockouts. On August 14, 1976, he lost to former world heavyweight champion George Foreman. On October 22, 1977, LeDoux battled Leon Spinks to a 10-round draw. LeDoux never officially fought Muhammad Ali, but the two did square off in a five-round exhibition for charity on December 5, 1977. Ali promised LeDoux a title fight, but Ali was defeated by Spinks and could no longer fulfill his promise.

LeDoux's most infamous fight occurred on February 13, 1977, against Johnny Boudreaux. After the eight-round fight, LeDoux and his trainer thought he had clearly won, but the decision was unanimously awarded to Boudreaux. While Boudreaux was interviewed on live television by ABC Sports personality Howard Cosell, LeDoux shouted at Cosell, "Tell it like it is," one of Cosell's famous catchphrases. Then LeDoux tried to kick Boudreaux, who jumped out of the way. Boudreaux's feet got tangled in the cord to Cosell's headset, and he accidentally pulled the headset off—along with Cosell's toupee.

LeDoux regretted his outburst. Cosell interviewed him, and LeDoux said, "I made a fool of myself." LeDoux later suggested that he'd been warned not to take the fight because it was rigged. In an interview many years later, LeDoux confessed that he kept a video of Cosell's toupee coming off. He said that he viewed it when he needed to have a "good laugh."

> *SATURDAY NIGHT LIVE* JABS MINNESOTA BOXER:

Duane Bobick was a successful professional boxer from Bowlus, Minnesota. In his first 38 matches, he was a perfect 38–0. On May 11, 1977, Bobick put his undefeated record to the test against Ken Norton at Madison Square Garden in New York City. Unfortunately for Bobick, he was dispatched in just 58 seconds in the first round by a technical knockout. (The referee decided that Bobick could no longer continue.) The fact that Bobick lost the fight in less than a minute was fodder for the popular sketch-comedy show *Saturday Night Live*. During the "Weekend Update" news sketch on May 14, 1977, the show poked fun at Bobick's speedy demise.

> MINNESOTA KICKS SOCCER TEAM FOLDS:

After losing money in four of the first five seasons, the Minnesota Kicks' original ownership group (page 220) sold the team in November 1980 to Ralph Sweet. Sweet bought the Kicks for a reported $1 million, almost double what the original owners had paid to buy the franchise from Denver. Sweet knew the team had lost nearly $800,000 the previous season but boldly declared that he had no intention of doing the same. After the 1981 outdoor season, rumors began to emerge that the franchise might fold. Attendance in 1981 had decreased by half from 1980, and the team lost $2.5 million. The Kicks' final game was played on September 6, 1981. We lost a playoff match to the Fort Lauderdale Strikers (the same Strikers who would move to Minnesota in 1983; see below) at Memorial Stadium on the U of M campus. Fans had no idea they were witnessing the end. Sweet made the decision to sell the team in mid-October and said that he would fold the club if a buyer could not be found. No deals were made, so it was decided that the team could sell some of the players' contracts. On December 8, 1981, a dispersal draft was held. Five Kicks players were chosen by other teams in the North American Soccer League. The other nine players became free agents. The dispersal draft officially put an end to the Kicks franchise.

Dan's Notes: From what I've gathered by asking those who were there, most fans weren't upset that we lost yet another sports franchise. They were upset that the pregame tailgating was over. The Kicks didn't charge for parking, so the parking lot often turned into quite a party.

❯ MINNESOTA STRIKERS LOSE CHAMPIONSHIP:

In the early 1980s, there were two soccer leagues. The North American Soccer League (NASL) held its season during the warm months, while the Major Indoor Soccer League (MISL) ran its season in winter.

The NASL's Fort Lauderdale Strikers moved to Minnesota in 1983 and became the Minnesota Strikers. Following the 1984

NASL season, a deal was reached between the two soccer leagues that allowed NASL teams to also play in the MISL, with hopes of increasing interest in soccer in the U.S. The Strikers began playing indoor games at Met Center in November. The TV commercials featured a catchy jingle: "Minnesota Strikers! Great balls of fire!"

Unfortunately, many NASL teams began to fold. On March 28, 1985, the NASL suspended operations because only the Strikers and one other team remained. The Strikers became strictly an indoor team. We made the MISL playoffs in each of our four seasons. In 1986, our team advanced to the MISL Championship Series against the San Diego Sockers. On May 26, 1986, the Strikers lost Game 7 of the series, 5–3, and the championship went to San Diego. As the *Star Tribune's* Susan Feyder put it, the Strikers had joined the club of Minnesota teams to lose championships.

In the 1988 season, the Strikers were eliminated from the playoffs on May 15 by the Cleveland Force. We lost the game, 7–2, and we lost the series four games to one. It was the last game the Strikers ever played. The team was dissolved due to financial difficulties.

Dan's Notes: I went to quite a few Strikers games at Met Center. Tino Lettieri was my favorite player. As a good luck charm, he kept a stuffed parrot named Ozzie in the net. The Strikers sold stuffed Ozzies at the souvenir stand and, of course, I had one.

SPORTS BOOKS FOR THE WHOLE FAMILY TO ENJOY

Adam Thielen
Football biography
$12.95 retail

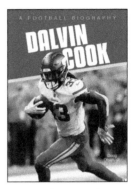

Dalvin Cook
Football biography
$12.95 retail

**Hockey Moms
Aren't Crazy**
Stories and jokes
$9.95 retail

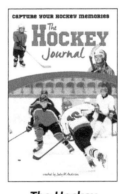

**The Hockey
Journal**
Stats & memories
$9.95 retail

Save the Season
Choose-your-path
interactive story
$9.95 retail

DAN'S THANKS

Going through countless old newspaper articles gave me a newfound respect for all the writers—specifically the Minnesota ones—who have contributed to documenting sports in our state. I appreciate all of their time, effort, knowledge, and experience. Some of them have even actively contributed to this project. Without them, this book would not be possible, and I honestly cannot thank them enough.

Special thanks to Dan Barreiro, Justin Gaard, Lou Nanne, Scott Korzenowski, Judd Zulgad, Patrick Reusse, Howard Sinker, Derek Felska (@CreaseAndAssist), VintageMnHockey.com, Ali Siddiqui, Stew Thornley, Nate Wells (@GopherState), Tony Tengwell, Matt Johnson (The Twins Almanac), Danny Cunningham, Ryan Jacobson, @1960sSports, Jeff Munneke, and Ross Brendel.

Calendar contributors: Will Ragatz, Anthony Paray, @TwinsWild16, @Michael_J_Adair, coworkers (Paul P., Michelle A., MC, KG, JD), Andy J., Dan L., TSCF, Keith Grinde, Jeff Haff, @Brand842, Ricky Cobb (@Super70sSports), @bstoffel350, @MrZMovies, and @mnannouncerguy.

Project contributors: Tim Mahoney, GB Leighton, Tina Schlieske, HelloBooking (The Billys), and Michael Shynes.

Additional thanks to Chris Hawkey, KFAN, SKOR North, KSTP, WCCO, KARE11, FOX 9, TPT, MPR, the *Star Tribune*, and the *Pioneer Press*.

SOURCES

Game data and player statistics were verified using the following websites:
- Baseball Reference (baseball-reference.com).
- Basketball Reference (basketball-reference.com).
- Hockey Reference (hockey-reference.com).
- Pro Football Reference (pro-football-reference.com).

"2019 Big Ten Men's Ice Hockey Tournament." Big Ten Conference (bigten.org). Accessed June 8, 2020.

Aldridge, David. "The Lakers plane crash that wasn't." ESPN (espn.com). January 24, 2000.

Allen, Kevin. "Houston and Cincinnati in NHL? It almost happened in 1977 when WHA-NHL talked merger." *USA Today* (usatoday.com). March 29, 2019.

Anderson, Dave. "The Mistaken Power of Billy Martin." *The New York Times.* July 24, 1975.

Apgar, Sally. "A deal on thin ice." *Star Tribune* (newspapers.com). February 1, 1993.

Armour, Mark, and Levitt, Dan. "A History of the MLBPA's Collective Bargaining Agreement: Part 3." The Hardball Times (fangraphs.com). November 9, 2016.

Aschburner, Steve. *Star Tribune* (newspapers.com).
- "NBA restores one Wolves draft pick." December 29, 2001.
- "McHale, Taylor accept NBA suspensions in Smith case." December 9, 2000.
- "Wolves admit to violation." September 9, 2000.
- "It's a deal: Rider's history." July 24, 1996.
- "Rider's ejection comes quickly; exit doesn't." March 11, 1996.
- "Frustrated Rider makes his case." December 13, 1994.
- "Wilson's solid performance puts QB controversy to rest." January 18, 1988.
- "Minnesota's back in the NBA." April 23, 1987.

Associated Press. ESPN (espn.com).
- "Caterer turns tables on Moss." November 4, 2010.
- "Vikings, Broncos both see season come to close." December 30, 2007.
- "After some confusion, Vikings select Bryant McKinnie." April 20, 2002.
- "Green, Vikings agree to buyout." January 4, 2002.

Associated Press. *Minneapolis Tribune* (newspapers.com).
- "Raging LeDoux kicks at boxer who beat him." February 14, 1977.
- "LA Says Lakers Can Use Arena." April 27, 1960.

Associated Press. *St. Cloud Times* (newspapers.com).
- "Vikings woo Berrian, acquire 2 others." March 1, 2008.
- "Met Stadium demolished." January 29, 1985.
- "Carew upset over negotiations, may demand trade." March 27, 1978.

Associated Press. *Star Tribune* (newspapers.com).
- "Faust leaves the Irish with his head high." November 27, 1985.
- "Strikers, 3 other NASL teams join indoor league." August 29, 1984.
- "Gophers, Five Others Form New Ice Loop." March 9, 1959.

Associated Press. "Baseball strike 'technically' ends after judge's ruling."
The Courier-Journal (newspapers.com). April 1, 1995.

Associated Press. "Belcher Won't Sign." *St. Louis Post-Dispatch*
(newspapers.com). January 10, 1984.

Associated Press. "Browns Trade Jim Marshall to Vikings." *The Logan Daily News*
(newspapers.com). September 13, 1961.

Associated Press. "College Hockey Loop Breaks Up." *The Pantograph*
(newspapers.com). March 15, 1958.

Associated Press. "Vikings Owners Split Between Grant, Van Brocklin." *Stevens
Point Daily Journal* (newspapers.com). January 18, 1961.

Associated Press. "Wolverines, MSC in New Hockey Loop." *Detroit Free Press*
(newspapers.com). November 29, 1951.

Augustoviz, Roman. *Star Tribune* (newspapers.com).
- "Gophers leaving WCHA to form Big Ten hockey." March 22, 2011.
- "Kicks players don't believe franchise will collapse." October 21, 1981.

Baca, Maria Elena. "Ceremonial shoveling begins." *Star Tribune*
(newspapers.com). August 31, 2007.

Banks, Don. *Star Tribune* (newspapers.com).
- "For Clancy, ending is an unhappy one." May 21, 1998.
- "Green's attack on Vikings owners puts his job in jeopardy."
  October 25, 1997.

Barreiro, Dan. *Star Tribune* (newspapers.com).
- "Only one man to blame, folks." January 15, 2001.
- "Stars playing in Minnesota makes no sense." December 10, 1993.
- "Sign of the times for Stars: Why?" April 14, 1993.
- "Team passes chemistry test." June 16, 1989.
- "Letterman-perfect." August 15, 1987.

Barreiro, Dan. Interview with Jack Morris. *Bumper to Bumper with Dan Barreiro*:
KFAN 100.3 FM. June 19, 2018.

Barstool Sports. "The Vikings Love Boat." YouTube (youtube.com).
March 12, 2018.

Batson, Larry. *Minneapolis Tribune* (newspapers.com).
- "No. 10 touched the lives of most of us; we won't forget him." May 9, 1979.
- "Blyleven proves free enterprise still works." June 2, 1976.

Beard, Gordon. "Orioles rally to scuttle Indians." *The Marion Star* (newspapers.com). April 29, 1985.

Beckmann, Jeffrey. "50 Players with the Most Swagger in MLB History." Bleacher Report (bleacherreport.com). August 22, 2011.

Berg, Steve. *Star Tribune* (newspapers.com).
- "Triad wants baseball but is reluctant to pay for it." October 4, 1997.
- "Fans loyal but some fear 'Minnesota Syndrome' as Kicks boot the big one." August 29, 1976.

Bergman, Jeremy. "Ravens trade kicker Kaare Vedvik to Vikings for pick." NFL (nfl.com). August 11, 2019.

"Best General Managers in Sports." *Forbes* (forbes.com). March 2, 2007.

Bierig, Joel. *Minneapolis Star and Tribune* (newspapers.com).
- "Griffith denies he plans to sell team." May 13, 1982.
- "Wynegar, Erickson traded to Yankees." May 13, 1982.
- "Vikings weren't music to Nelson's ears." April 28, 1982.

Blackburn, Pete. CBS Sports (cbssports.com).
- "Hurricanes winger Andrei Svechnikov pulls off lacrosse-style goal for second time." December 17, 2019.
- "NBA Draft Lottery 2019: Conspiracy theories that make us wonder if the lottery is rigged." May 14, 2019.

Blount, Rachel. *Star Tribune* (newspapers.com).
- "Big Ten buzzkill." February 28, 2016.
- "'U' nets Lucia." April 10, 1999.
- "Fans won't allow DeBus to forget Legg's goal." November 29, 1996.
- "Just like the old days for Stars, fans." December 10, 1993.
- "Stars' Game 2 jinx continues." May 18, 1991.

Blum, Ronald. "Baseball revenue sharing goes to prospects." *The Daily Journal* (newspapers.com). May 18, 2004.

Bollinger, Rhett. Major League Baseball (mlb.com).
- "Twins introduce front-office duo Falvey, Levine." November 7, 2016.
- "Ryan reflects on releasing Papi in 2003." February 2, 2016.

BoxRec (boxrec.com).
- "Duane Bobick." Accessed June 7, 2020.
- "Scott LeDoux." Accessed June 7, 2020.

Brackin, Dennis. *Star Tribune* (newspapers.com).
- "LeDoux's connection with Ali, in and out of the ring." June 5, 2016.
- "NCAA penalizes 'U' for violations." March 28, 1991.
- "Georgia Tech holds off Gophers in Southeast Regional final." March 26, 1990.
- "Backcourt play helps 'U' shoot down Syracuse, reach final 8." March 24, 1990.

- "Convicted of assault, Ciccarelli gets day in jail and $1000 fine."
  August 25, 1988.
- "'U' basketball team placed on probation for 2 years by NCAA."
  March 8, 1988.
- "NCAA chats with 'U.'" February 8, 1988.
- "Niekro given 10-day penalty." August 6, 1987.
- "Did Niekro mean to give Angels a rough time? League officials will rule."
  August 5, 1987.
- "Niekro gets in a scrape, but Twins roll." August 4, 1987.
- "North Stars ousted by Edmonton." May 2, 1984.
- "Stars rally fails; Oilers lead 2–0." April 27, 1984.

Brackin, Dennis, and Furst, Randy. "Wilderson is stripped of control."
Star Tribune (newspapers.com). July 6, 1988.

Brackin, Dennis, and Neal III, La Velle E. "Forecast for Twins is cloudy and
uncertain." *Star Tribune* (newspapers.com). December 18, 2000.

Briere, Tom. *Minneapolis Tribune* (newspapers.com).
- "Twins' choice looks for bonus." June 7, 1983.
- "Twins await Yankee offer on Carew." January 20, 1979.
- "Allen's 2 inside-park homers subdue Twins." August 1, 1972.
- "Pipers Return to Pittsburgh." July 22, 1969.
- "T-C Group Awarded NHL Franchise." February 10, 1966.
- "Dodgers Land in Twinsville, Well Armed." October 5, 1965.
- "Lakers' Move to Los Angeles Gets NBA OK." April 28, 1960.

Broome, Anthony. "Rocky Balboa statue gets a Minnesota Vikings makeover."
CBS Sports (cbssports.com). January 21, 2018.

Brothers, Bruce. *Minneapolis Tribune* (newspapers.com).
- "Kicks stumble; Strikers win." September 7, 1981.
- "Strikers give Kicks a defeat to remember." September 3, 1981.
- "Kicks stun Tulsa 3–1 in playoff." August 23, 1981.
- "Kicks' owner pledges activism." November 13, 1980.

Brown, Curt. "Shameful night in U sports history." *Star Tribune*
(newspapers.com). January 22, 2017.

Brown, Maury. "Revenue Sharing Making an Impact." Baseball America
(baseballamerica.com). March 2, 2010.

"Bud Grant." Winnipeg Blue Bombers (bluebombers.com).
Accessed May 30, 2020.

Buha, Jovan. "Here's the story behind that Sam Cassell 'Big Balls' dance."
The Athletic (theathletic.com). February 12, 2019.

Bujer's Sports Classics. "2006 Minnesota vs Texas Tech – Insight Bowl." YouTube
(youtube.com). September 19, 2018.

Byrod, Fred. "Jet Jaunt Keeps Warriors on Move." *The Philadelphia Enquirer* (newspapers.com). January 29, 1960.

Cafardo, Nick. "Former Twins GM still regrets releasing David Ortiz." *Boston Globe* (bostonglobe.com). April 4, 2015.

Cameron, Linda A. "The making of Minnesota's Metropolitan Stadium." MinnPost (minnpost.com). September 27, 2016.

Chanen, David. *Star Tribune* (newspapers.com).
- "Final Vikings cruise cases resolved." May 27, 2006.
- "Ex-Viking convicted on one count." April 21, 2006.

Chanen, David; McEnroe, Paul; and Seifert, Kevin. "Vikings cruise was allegedly a sex party." *Star Tribune* (newspapers.com). October 12, 2005.

Chanen, David, and Zulgad, Judd. "Culpepper, 3 other Vikings are charged." *Star Tribune* (newspapers.com). December 16, 2005.

Christensen, Joe. *Star Tribune* (newspapers.com).
- "Torii: 'I didn't want to leave.'" November 23, 2007.
- "Nishioka's release gives Twins relief." September 29, 2012.
- "'Sorry' state of affairs." April 8, 2011.
- "Twins get top bid for Japanese infielder." November 27, 2010.

Coffey, Jerry. "Television's candid cameras get few smiles from pitcher." *Fort Worth Star-Telegram* (newspapers.com). June 9, 1976.

Coleman, Jim. "Prep Star Makes Hit in Pros." *Los Angeles Times* (newspapers.com). October 13, 1983.

Coleman, Nick. "Griffith spares few targets in Waseca remarks." *Minneapolis Tribune* (newspapers.com). October 1, 1978.

Craig, Mark. "Wide receiver Williamson is on his own vision quest." *Star Tribune* (newspapers.com). May 23, 2007.

Craig, Mark, and McDaniel, Randall. *100 Things Vikings Fans Should Know and Do Before They Die.* Triumph Books. October 1, 2016.

Croman, John. "I've Been Wondering: *Ski-U-Mah?*" KARE 11 (kare11.com). April 1, 2007.

Cronin, Courtney. "Vikings fire OC John DeFilippo." ESPN (espn.com). December 11, 2018.

Cullum, Dick. *Minneapolis Tribune* (newspapers.com).
- "Bobick follows his plan, TKOs LeDoux in 8th." July 29, 1977.
- "Bobick tops LeDoux for 35th victory." April 23, 1976.
- "LeDoux, D. Bobick win bouts." April 24, 1975.
- "Incidentally, a Great Play." July 11, 1968.
- "Tark Isn't Van Brocklin's 'Type.'" February 11, 1967.
- "Area Can Support Big-League Team." June 17, 1953.

Cusick, Kevin. "Classic Minnesota Vikings video: Mud Bowl '77." *Pioneer Press* (twincities.com). August 20, 2012.

Davenport, Gary. "A Brief History of the NFL Supplemental Draft." Bleacher Report (bleacherreport.com). July 10, 2013.

DePass, Dee; Zulgad, Judd; and McGrath, Dennis. "Down it came." *Star Tribune* (newspapers.com). December 13, 2010.

Diaz, Kevin, and Zavoral, Nolan. "'U' official says nearly $200,000 went to 17 students." *Star Tribune* (newspapers.com). April 22, 1988.

Dohrmann, George. "U basketball program accused of academic fraud." *Pioneer Press* (twincities.com). March 10, 1999.

Duchschere, Kevin, and Pate, Eric T. "Fans party heartily to the bitter end." *Star Tribune* (newspapers.com). April 14, 1993.

Ettel Gonzalez, Diana. "Ciccarelli changes his plea to guilty." *Star Tribune* (newspapers.com). January 21, 1988.

Fahy, Claire. "Remembering John Wooden's legacy." *Daily Bruin* (dailybruin.com). February 25, 2015.

Felska, Derek. "A Look Back: The Definitive History of Why the Minnesota North Stars Left." *The Sports Daily* (thesportsdaily.com). March 10, 2019.

Feyder, Susan. "Strikers join club, disappoint fans in big game." *Minneapolis Star and Tribune* (newspapers.com). May 27, 1986.

"Five NHL team records that may never be matched." National Hockey League (nhl.com). January 12, 2016.

Foley, Ellen, and Zgoda, Jerry. "Dino Ciccarelli faces charge of indecent exposure." *Star Tribune* (newspapers.com). November 28, 1987.

Fowler, Bob. *Minneapolis Tribune* (newspapers.com).
- "Van Brocklin's Resignation Stuns Vikings." February 12, 1967.
- "Fran Tarkenton Quits Vikings." February 11, 1967.
- "Gossett's Field Goals Spark L.A." November 21, 1966.

Fox, Steve. "Strike 8, baseball's out." *Tucson Citizen* (newspapers.com). August 12, 1994.

Fox Sports North. "Wolves look to end draft lottery losing streak." Fox Sports (foxsports.com). May 13, 2019.

foxboy1. "Norm Sucks." YouTube (youtube.com). September 18, 2009.

Frederick, Jace. "Changing of the guards." *Pioneer Press* (twincities.com). July 1, 2017.

Furst, Randy. *Star Tribune* (newspapers.com).
- "Twins believe they'll play." February 5, 2002.

- "Play ball, court tells Twins." January 23, 2002.
- "Judge orders Twins to play in Metrodome in 2002." November 17, 2001.

Furst, Randy, and Hotakainen, Rob. "Grand jury indicts Darville in theft of $186,000 from University of Minnesota." *Star Tribune* (newspapers.com). May 26, 1988.

Furst, Randy, and Seifert, Kevin. "Moss charged with Marijuana possession." *Star Tribune* (newspapers.com). October 2, 2002.

Furst, Randy; Whereatt, Robert; and Banaszynski, Jacqui. "It's beat the clock to fix the roof." *Minneapolis Star and Tribune* (newspapers.com). December 31, 1982.

Gallagher, Tim. "Carroll court named for basketball team's safe crash landing." *Sioux City Journal* (siouxcityjournal.com). September 11, 2010.

Gallen, Daniel. "Derek Barnett, the Philadelphia Eagles' prize in the Sam Bradford trade, comes up big vs. Minnesota Vikings." Penn Live (pennlive.com). January 22, 2018.

Gates, Christopher. "Minnesota Vikings' Worst Draft Pick Ever – Dimitrius Underwood." SB Nation: Daily Norseman (dailynorseman.com). April 16, 2011.

Gelb, Matt. "Club enlists a former GM to scout." *The Philadelphia Enquirer* (newspapers.com). December 1, 2016.

Genovese, Chico. "Garvey to Michigan State." *The Tampa Times* (newspapers.com). June 7, 1966.

Gilbert, John. *Star Tribune* (newspapers.com).
- "Freshman is good as gold for Gophers." March 24, 1996.
- "Process baffles Brooks." June 23, 1988.
- "North Stars take off kid gloves to gain league lead in penalties." February 27, 1981.
- "St. Paul team is named the Saints." August 19, 1976.
- "Area soccer fans get their Kicks when pro team starts play in April." January 29, 1976.
- "Professional soccer comes to Minnesota." November 26, 1975.
- "Musselman signs to coach San Diego in ABA." July 29, 1975.

Gilbert, John, and Swanson, Merrill. "'U' considers Ashland coach Bill Musselman." *Minneapolis Tribune* (newspapers.com). April 5, 1971.

Glaser, Kyle. "World Series Champion Opening Day Payroll Ranks in the Wild Card Era." Baseball America (baseballamerica.com). October 31, 2019.

Goessling, Ben. "Treadwell, Vedvik, Sloter among Vikings' final cuts." *Star Tribune* (newspapers.com). September 1, 2019.

Goldstein, Richard. "Calvin Griffith, 87, Is Dead; Tight-Fisted Baseball Owner." *The New York Times* (nytimes.com). October 21, 1999.

"Gopher Basketball 1971–72 Season." GopherHole (gopherhole.com). Accessed May 25, 2020.

Gordon, Dick. *Minneapolis Star* (newspapers.com).
- "Big Ten may slap Gophers for brawl." January 26, 1972.
- "'Nicklaus is blind man.'" June 13, 1970.
- "'Felt I Belonged Here,' Explains Cowles; Ambition Realized." May 15, 1948.
- "Crisler: Will Not Stand in Cowles' Way." April 28, 1948.

Green, Taylor. "Kansas City Chiefs: 10 Biggest Draft Busts in Team History." Bleacher Report (bleacherreport.com). April 12, 2011.

Grow, Doug. *Star Tribune* (newspapers.com).
- "Stars' 5–3 loss at home not in script." May 22, 1991.
- "With Lemieux out, Stars play to the crowd in 3–1 win." May 20, 1991.
- "Stars lose game, but win respect." April 27, 1984.

Green, Norm. "The 35 Biggest Moments in Modern Dallas History: The North Stars Move to Dallas." *D Magazine* (dmagazine.com). December 16, 2009.

Guregian, Karen. "Randy Moss, ownership at odds." *Boston Herald* (bostonherald.com). October 7, 2010.

Haga, Chuck, and Zavoral, Nolan. "Wilderson resigns, plans to return to teaching." *Star Tribune* (newspapers.com). December 9, 1988.

Hartman, Sid. *Star Tribune* (newspapers.com).
- "Ryan, Smith had a hand in building Twins success." September 29, 2019.
- "Molitor remains out of baseball for now." March 14, 2019.
- "Wooden missed chance to coach at U." June 6, 2010.
- "Jottings." August 14, 1999.
- "Jottings." January 13, 1997.
- "Wolfenson sets March 1 deadline." December 7, 1993.
- "Jottings." February 11, 1989.
- "It's Bud–Chapter 2." December 19, 1984.
- "Sid Hartman" (column). December 18, 1984.
- "Sid Hartman" (column). March 6, 1984.
- "Steckel to coach Vikings." January 29, 1984.
- "Swift back to school." September 3, 1983.
- "Sid Hartman" (column). April 28, 1982.
- "Gophers to Metrodome." April 11, 1982.
- "Sid Hartman" (column). February 4, 1979.
- "Twins satisfy Carew, trade him to Angels." February 4, 1979.
- "Carew Upset." February 2, 1979.
- "Carew to visit San Francisco." January 5, 1979.
- "Carew rejects Giants; Twins get Koosman." December 9, 1978.
- "Sid Hartman" (column). May 28, 1978.
- "Sid Hartman" (column). May 14, 1978.
- "Sid Hartman" (column). March 27, 1978.
- "Ryan leaves." March 1, 1978.
- "Grant seeks coach." February 28, 1978.

- "Vikings coaches to Bears?" February 18, 1978.
- "Will Carew be chased?" February 12, 1978.
- "Tarkenton breaks ankle, is out for year." November 14, 1977.
- "NCAA lifts indefinite probation on 'U.'" November 8, 1977.
- "Twins trade Blyleven, Thompson for 4 Rangers." June 2, 1976.
- "Violation discussed." December 19, 1975.
- "NCAA alleges 'U' basketball violations." July 24, 1975.
- "Sid Hartman" (column). July 23, 1975.
- "Finks gets high position with Bears." September 13, 1974.
- "Winter denies he, Finks had been feuding." May 21, 1974.
- "Finks resigns from Vikings; ownership desire called reason." May 20, 1974.
- "Sid Hartman" (column). January 28, 1972.
- "Hill's Remarks Cost Him $150." June 21, 1970.
- "Kapp: Chiefs Like Redwoods." January 12, 1970.
- "Martin Won't Be Re-Hired." October 13, 1969.
- "Boswell: Trying to Make Me a Bad Wolf." August 11, 1969.
- "Killebrew May Be Lost Six Weeks." July 10, 1968.
- "Hartman's Roundup." February 11, 1967.
- "Winnipeg Pro Team Names Grant Coach." January 4, 1957.
- "Vancisin, Herkal in as Aids." June 30, 1948.

Hartman, Sid, and Bierig, Joel. "Twins trade Wilfong, Corbett." *Minneapolis Star and Tribune* (newspapers.com). May 12, 1982.

Hartman, Sid, and Libman, Gary. "Rod Carew balks at effort to trade him to Giants." *Minneapolis Tribune* (newspapers.com). December 8, 1978.

Hartman, Sid, with Rippel, Joel A. *Sid Hartman's Great Minnesota Sports Moments.* MVP Books. October 24, 2008.

Hartman, Sid, and Roe, Jon. "Holtz happy at 'U' but . . ." *Star Tribune* (newspapers.com). November 25, 1985.

Hartman, Sid; Smetanka, Mary Jane; and Doyle, Pat. "'U' weighing fate of 4 players." *Star Tribune* (newspapers.com). March 11, 1999.

Harvey, Randy. "Thanks to a Blizzard, Gophers Missed a Wizard." *The Los Angeles Times* (newspapers.com). March 24, 1997.

Hazeltine National. Hazeltine National Golf Club (hazeltinenational.com).
- "Historic Hazeltine: 1966 U.S. Women's Open Championship." September 23, 2016.
- "Historic Hazeltine: Remembering the 1991 U.S. Open Championship at Hazeltine." June 16, 2016.

Hengen, Bill. *The Minneapolis Star* (newspapers.com).
- "New Viking Coach Takes Firm Grasp of Herculean Situation." January 19, 1961.
- "Grant Says He Is Not Viking Grid Candidate." January 18, 1961.

Hickok, Lorena A. "16,000 Fans, 'Lost' in the Immense Structure, Watch Gophers Win." *Minneapolis Tribune* (newspapers.com). October 5, 1924.

Highkin, Sean. "The bizarre saga of Joe Smith's illegal Minnesota Timberwolves contract." *For the Win* (ftw.usatoday.com). January 9, 2014.

Hine, Chris. "Butler levels scathing critique, confronting teammates, GM." *Star Tribune* (newspapers.com). October 11, 2018.

"History of Hazeltine." Hazeltine National Golf Club (hazeltinenational.com). Accessed May 25, 2020.

Holbert, Allan. *Minneapolis Tribune* (newspapers.com).
- "Dallas vanquishes Vikings 23–6." January 2, 1978.
- "Perhaps this is a rebuilding year for the Vikings." November 13, 1977.
- "Kicks lose Soccer Bowl 3–0." August 29, 1976.
- "Saints fold, but club status still uncertain." February 29, 1976.
- "Cowboys finish Vikings 17–14." December 29, 1975.
- "Steelers stop Vikings cold 16–6." January 13, 1975.

Hotakainen, Rob, and Furst, Randy. "Sauer's bold move sparks anger, surprise." *Star Tribune* (newspapers.com). July 6, 1988.

Hruby, Patrick. "The coolest goal ever scored in hockey." ESPN (espn.com). April 8, 2010.

"Hubert H. Humphrey Metrodome." This Great Game (thisgreatgame.com). Accessed May 25, 2020.

Hugunin, Marc, and Thornley, Stew. *Minnesota Hoops: Basketball in the North Star State*. Minnesota Historical Society Press. September 28, 2006.

Isola, Frank. "Spree: Offer is 'insult.'" *Daily News* (newspapers.com). November 1, 2004.

Jackson, Barry; Walters, Charley; and Wittenmyer, Gordon. "Expos, Twins may be eliminated, report says." *The Times Leader* (newspapers.com). October 26, 2001.

Jaffe, Chris. "40th anniversary: two Dick Allen inside-the-park homers." The Hardball Times (fangraphs.com). July 31, 2012.

Jensen, Sean. "And the buyer of the 'Whizzinator' is . . ." *Pioneer Press* (twincities.com). August 29, 2009.

Johnson, Charles. "Cities Hit Homer!" *The Minneapolis Star* (newspapers.com). October 27, 1960.

Johnson, Rod. "Garvey County Batting Champ." *The Tampa Times* (newspapers.com). April 28, 1966.

Jones, Dean. "The lasting legacy of former Vikings receiver Randy Moss." Fansided: The Viking Age (thevikingage.com). February 13, 2020.

Jones, Jack. "Super Bowl Spread History: Vegas Odds for Every Game." BetFirm (betfirm.com). February 5, 2020.

Kaszuba, Mike, and Brunswick, Mark. "U gets stadium; Twins on track." *Star Tribune* (newspapers.com). May 21, 2006.

Kay, Alex. "2018 NFL Playoff Odds: Philadelphia Eagles vs. Minnesota Vikings NFC Championship Game Expert Picks." *Forbes* (forbes.com). January 21, 2018.

Keenan, Jimmy. "October 4, 1969: Orioles win first-ever ALCS game." Society for American Baseball Research (sabr.org). Accessed May 21, 2020.

Kennedy, Patrick. "Potential buyers get head start on making preliminary offers." *Star Tribune* (newspapers.com). June 21, 1997.

Kennedy, Tony. "Twins: Watkins isn't in game." *Star Tribune* (newspapers.com). May 2, 2002.

Kenyon, David. "The Top 10 NFL Defenses of All Time." Bleacher Report (bleacherreport.com). August 6, 2018.

King, Peter. "Letting Go." *Sports Illustrated* Vault (vault.si.com). March 20, 2000.

Klauda, Paul. *Star Tribune* (newspapers.com).
- "Minority program director at university fired." April 23, 1988.
- "Souvenir-hunting at Met leads to charges." December 21, 1981.

Korzenowski, Scott. "Fight for your Right." *Korzo on Sunday Mornings* (kfan.com). January 26, 2020.

Krawczynski, John. "'Home' again." *Winona Daily News* (newspapers.com). October 8, 2010.

Levitt, Zak. *30 for 30: Bad Boys*. ESPN Films. April 17, 2014.

Levy, Paul. "Scott Ledoux: Still fighting." *Star Tribune* (startribune.com). November 18, 2007.

Libman, Gary. *Minneapolis Tribune* (newspapers.com).
- "Angry Carew vows he will not play for Griffith's Twins again." October 2, 1978.
- "Carew to stay with Twins a spell longer." June 15, 1978.
- "Twins relent, sign Marshall, then lose 4–2." May 14, 1978.
- "Carew says he will never sign again with the Twins." May 13, 1978.
- "Smalley traded to the Yankees." April 11, 1982.
- "NCAA penalties on 'U' temporarily lifted." December 3, 1976.
- "'U' won't declare three cage stars ineligible." May 6, 1976.

Lindley, Bob. "Bert's Gesture 'Not Obscene.'" *Fort Worth Star-Telegram* (newspapers.com). June 8, 1976.

Lingo, Will. "Top 10 MLB Draft Holdouts of All-Time." Baseball America (baseballamerica.com). July 25, 2014.

Lopresti, Mike. "With no explanation, Holtz leaves the Irish." *St. Cloud Times* (newspapers.com). November 20, 1996.

Lundegaard, Bob. "Then the Vikes' Balloon Burst." *Minneapolis Tribune* (newspapers.com). January 12, 1970.

Maki, Allan. "Big, Bad Goldie." The Globe and Mail (theglobeandmail.com). July 30, 2002.

Manza Young, Shalise. "Buildup to the breaking point." *The Boston Globe* (newspapers.com). October 10, 2010.

McGrath, Dennis J. *Star Tribune* (newspapers.com).
- "Officials annoyed by wasted risk, work." May 24, 1994.
- "Deflation may have saved dome from major rip." April 16, 1983.

McGowen, Deane. "Boudreaux Beats LeDoux." *The New York Times* (nytimes.com). February 14, 1977.

McKenna, Charley. *Star Tribune* (newspapers.com).
- "NASL suspends operations for 1985." March 29, 1985.
- "Vikings' Marshall announces retirement." December 5, 1979.

Meador, Ron. "Ice rips dome; damage believed to be modest." *Minneapolis Star and Tribune* (newspapers.com). April 15, 1983.

"Men's Division I Hockey Attendance." USCHO (uscho.com). Accessed June 8, 2020.

"Men's Ice Hockey." Holy Cross Crusaders (goholycross.com). Accessed June 7, 2020.

"Metropolitan Stadium." American Football Database (americanfootballdatabase.fandom.com). Accessed June 6, 2020.

"Metropolitan Stadium, Bloomington, 1956." Society for American Baseball Research (sabr.org). Accessed June 6, 2020.

Millea, John, and Hartman, Sid. "Twins agree to stay put at least two more years." *Star Tribune* (newspapers.com). July 23, 1998.

Miller, Phil. *Star Tribune* (newspapers.com).
- "Falvey more than happy to keep Molitor at helm." November 8, 2016.
- "Forced out at home." July 19, 2016.
- "Twins offer Molitor managerial reins." November 2, 2014.
- "Win-loss math forced GM to make a move that severed longtime ties." September 30, 2014.

Minneapolis Star (newspapers.com).
- "U keeps pre-game drill." January 29, 1972.
- "Fly This Plane, Jim: We'll Wind Up In Hawaii." October 26, 1964.
- "State Pro Gridders Baptized 'Vikings.'" September 27, 1960.
- "Wooden to UCLA; Off Minnesota List." April 20, 1948.

Minneapolis Tribune (newspapers.com).
- "Vikings officially out of playoffs." December 20, 1981.
- "5 Kicks players find new teams in NASL draft." December 8, 1981.
- "U of M takes NCAA to high court." October 29, 1977.
- "WHA votes St. Paul franchise." August 10, 1976.
- "Miami Crushes Vikings 24–7." January 14, 1974.
- "Bomb Calls Clear Stadium, 7 Buildings." August 26, 1970.
- "Mays, N.L. Edge A.L. 1–0." July 10, 1968.
- "NHL Club Named the 'North Stars.'" May 26, 1966.
- "Lakers Have a Happy Landing." January 19, 1960.
- "'Metropolitan Stadium' Is Now Official Name." July 20, 1956.
- "'U' Football Fans to Get First View of Stadium Today." October 4, 1924.

"Minnesota Fighting Saints History (1972–1977)." Vintage Minnesota Hockey (vintagemnhockey.com). Accessed April 23, 2020.

"Minnesota Kicks Franchise History (1976–1981)." Stats Crew (statscrew.com). Accessed June 7, 2020.

[Minnesota Kicks Games]. SoccerStats.us (soccerstats.us). Accessed June 6, 2020.

"Minnesota Timberwolves Playoff History." Real GM (basketball.realgm.com). Accessed April 4, 2020.

Minnesota Vikings. "Full Game: Minneapolis Miracle, Minnesota Vikings vs. New Orleans Saints, 2017 NFC Divisional Round." YouTube (youtube.com). March 23, 2020.

"Minnesota Wild Team History." Sports Team History (sportsteamhistory.com). Accessed April 24, 2020.

"MLB History: The Threat of Contraction Begins." Fox Sports (foxsports.com). June 30, 2017.

Mona, Dave. *Minneapolis Tribune* (newspapers.com).
- "Martin Wants Two Birds in the Hand." October 4, 1969.
- "Twins Win; Oliva Lost Rest of Year." September 1, 1968.

Moore, Janet, and Smith, Kelly. "Dome roof quietly bows out." *Star Tribune* (newspapers.com). January 19, 2014.

Murphy, Austin. "Gone But Not Forgotten." *Sports Illustrated* (si.com). December 20, 1993.

Myslenski, Skip, and Pierson, Don. "Ryan: I could work for Ditka." *Chicago Tribune* (newspapers.com). December 31, 1981.

Nanne, Lou. Personal Interview by Dan Whenesota. April 1, 2018.

NBA Advanced Stats. "Active Franchises." NBA (nba.com). Accessed April 4, 2020.

NBA TNT Tip-Off. TNT. October 16, 2018.

"NCAA Division I Ice Hockey Poll." *The Palm Beach Post* (newspapers.com). March 21, 2006.

"NCAA Tournament Pairwise Comparison Ratings." College Hockey News (CollegeHockeyNews.com). Accessed June 14, 2020.

Neal III, La Velle E. *Star Tribune* (newspapers.com).
- "Contract in hand, Nishioka takes in his new surroundings." December 18, 2010.
- "Lacking leverage, and timing." February 3, 2008.
- "Alabama businessman interested in Twins." November 25, 2001.
- "Pohlads ask staff to hang tight—for now." November 10, 2001.
- "Ortiz looking to break out of his spring slump." March 25, 1999.

Netland, Dwayne. *Minneapolis Tribune* (newspapers.com).
- "East All-Stars nip West 3–2." January 26, 1972.
- "Jacklin's 281 Wins Open by 7." June 22, 1970.
- "Golf" (column). June 20, 1970.
- "Golf" (column). June 19, 1970.
- "Stars Whip Seals 3–1." October 22, 1967.
- "1970 U.S. Open to Be Held at Hazeltine." January 29, 1967.
- "Zoilo Says Dodgers 'Got Every Break.'" October 15, 1965.

"NFC Championship History." Vegas Insider (vegasinsider.com). Accessed May 24, 2020.

NFL. YouTube (youtube.com).
- "1998 NFC Championship Game: Atlanta Falcons vs. Minnesota Vikings | NFL Full Game." YouTube (youtube.com). April 6, 2020.
- "Top 50 Sound FX | #24: WR Nate Poole's 2003 Game-Winning TD | NFL." November 13, 2015.

"'NFL 100 Greatest' No. 54: Minnesota Vikings defensive lineman Jim Marshall runs the wrong way for a safety." National Football League (nfl.com). Accessed May 24, 2020.

NFL Films. NFL (nfl.com).
- "#2 Earnest Byner's Fumble | NFL Films | Top 10 Worst Plays." October 14, 2016.
- "Super Bowl XI Recap: Raiders vs. Vikings." Accessed April 14, 2020.
- "Super Bowl IX Recap: Steelers vs. Vikings." Accessed April 14, 2020.
- "Super Bowl VIII Recap: Vikings vs. Dolphins." Accessed April 13, 2020.
- "Super Bowl IV Recap: Vikings vs. Chiefs." Accessed April 13, 2020.

NFL Films. "#5 Jim Marshall's Wrong Way Run | NFL Films | Top 10 Worst Plays." YouTube (youtube.com). October 14, 2016.

NFL Throwback. YouTube (youtube.com).
- "The Wildest QB Run in NFL History | NFL Vault Stories." September 6, 2018.
- "How One Drop in the '87 NFC Championship Changed the NFL Forever | NFL Vault Stories." November 10, 2017.

"NHL Jets sold, likely going to Minnesota." United Press International (upi.com). October 18, 1995.

Nichols, Max. *The Minneapolis Star* (newspapers.com).
- "Winter to Keep Control." August 24, 1974.
- "Two Cage Suspensions Are Just." January 29, 1972.

Nicklaus, Jack. "Trouble Lurks in Sylvan Glades." *Sports Illustrated* (si.com). June 15, 1970.

Olson, Rochelle. "At 10, Target Field has what it needs: A winning team." *Star Tribune* (newspapers.com). October 7, 2019.

Pasquarelli, Len. "Slow on trigger, Vikings miss pick." ESPN (espn.com). April 26, 2003.

Patt, Jason. "Sam Cassell's Big Balls Dance cost Timberwolves a title, says Flip Saunders." SB Nation (sbnation.com). November 4, 2014.

Perry, Dwight. "Just like the Lakers, Minnesota lost John Wooden to Los Angeles." *The Seattle Times* (seattletimes.com). October 8, 2009.

Pierce, Zack. "25 years ago today, Kirby Puckett became a World Series hero." Fox Sports (foxsports.com). November 15, 2016.

Pierson, Don. "Vikings losers in Underwood gamble." *Chicago Tribune* (chicagotribune.com). August 12, 1999.

Pierson, Don, and Rollow, Cooper. "Finks resigns as Bears' general manager." *Chicago Tribune* (newspapers.com). August 25, 1983.

Pinney, Gregor W. *Minneapolis Tribune* (newspapers.com).
- "Specific violations in university report on basketball scandal." March 11, 1976.
- "'U' reveals more penalties from NCAA." March 11, 1976.
- "U team gets 2 years of penalties." March 10, 1976.
- "'U' sports charges revealed; Magrath agrees to action." January 10, 1976.

Pro Football Hall of Fame (profootballhof.com).
- "Jim Finks." Accessed May 25, 2020.
- "The NFL's Largest Trade." Accessed April 12, 2020.

Pruitt, Chrissi. "McCombs' promise." *Star Tribune* (newspapers.com). July 3, 1998.

Rand, Michael. *Star Tribune* (newspapers.com).
- "KG wants to buy Timberwolves from Taylor." December 15, 2017.
- "Ex-Vikings WR Troy Williamson reflects on time in Minnesota, wanting to fight Brad Childress." June 28, 2016.
- "Still struggling to feed his family." February 11, 2016.
- "Happy 25th Rantiversary." November 5, 2014.

Reed, Jesse. "Reviewing the Complete Timeline of NFL, Saints Bountygate Scandal." Bleacher Report (bleacherreport.com). December 11, 2012.

Reeve, Tad. "Hazeltine grows up." *Pioneer Press* (twincities.com). August 11, 2009.

Reusse, Patrick. *Star Tribune* (newspapers.com).
- "Once an underdog, Butler's turned into an egomaniac." October 11, 2018.
- "You've come a long way, Big Papi." March 20, 2016.
- "Capitol naysayers play their last tired hand: fictitious financial ruin." May 22, 2006.
- "Gophers had a chance for big success in the Maroney Era." January 1, 2006.
- "For a while, we actually believed." October 11, 2003.
- "Pohlad family's vision is intact." January 17, 2002.
- "Wrong-way run an unhappy memory." January 24, 1999.
- "Twins have offer from Charlotte." September 7, 1997.
- "LeDoux remembers hair-raising Cosell tale." April 22, 1995.
- "Burns fuming at fans' curses." November 6, 1989.
- "Stein & company make quite a steal." June 16, 1989.

Rigert, Joe, and Hotakainen, Rob. "Darville letter says he did as ordered." *Star Tribune* (newspapers.com). June 10, 1988.

Rios Jr., Orly. "NFL Draft 2011: Did Minnesota Vikings Reach at No. 12 with Christian Ponder?" Bleacher Report (bleacherreport.com). April 28, 2011.

Rippel, Joel. "Bud Grant: Minnesota Sports Hall of Fame inductee, Class of 1987." *Star Tribune* (startribune.com). November 17, 2019.

Roe, Jon. *Star Tribune* (newspapers.com).
- "Money talks, Morris walks." December 19, 1991.
- "Strikers are sent packing by the Force." May 16, 1988.
- "Salem resigns as 'U' grid coach." October 26, 1983.
- "Huskers shuck Gophers 84–13." September 18, 1983.
- "A Sentimental 'Memorial' for the Brickhouse." November 20, 1981.
- "Gophers romp but Buckeyes win." September 16, 1979.
- "2 players declared ineligible by 'U.'" October 25, 1977.
- "'U' men's sports back on probation." August 4, 1977.
- "NCAA places all Gopher men's teams on probation." October 22, 1976.
- "Court order will allow Thompson to play." January 19, 1976.
- "Top 'U' basketball player is ineligible." January 17, 1976.
- "Buckeyes KO Gophers 50–44." January 26, 1972.
- "Pittsburgh's ABA Entry Moves Here." June 29, 1968.
- "Miami New Muskie Site." May 22, 1968.

Roe, Jon, and Hartman, Sid. "Morris, Twins make it official." *Star Tribune* (newspapers.com). February 6, 1991.

Roscher, Liz. "'You f---ing need me': Jimmy Butler reportedly practiced with Minnesota while cursing out team execs." Yahoo! Sports (sports.yahoo.com). October 10, 2018.

Rosenthal, Gregg. "Childress takes blame for 12 men in the huddle." NBC Sports: PFT (profootballtalk.nbcsports.com). January 27, 2010.

Russo, Michael. "Halfway into Parise-Suter deals, here's the full story of how it all went down." *The Athletic* (theathletic.com). January 7, 2019.

Russo, Michael. "North Star memories end in final, shining moment." *Star Tribune* (newspapers.com). April 11, 2010.

RyanMPLS. "Jerry Burns Uncensored - Minnesota Vikings." YouTube (youtube.com). Accessed May 31, 2020.

Salfino, Michael. "Memo to NFL GMs: Stop Drafting Kickers." FiveThirtyEight (fivethirtyeight.com). September 21, 2018.

Sansevere, Robert (Bob). *Star Tribune* (newspapers.com).
- "Schnelker speaks out." November 2, 1989.
- "Young breaks Vikings' tackles, hearts." October 31, 1988.
- "Montana to start where he left off against Vikings." October 29, 1988.
- "Vikings drop out of playoffs." January 18, 1988.
- "Bud Grant retires again as coach." January 7, 1986.
- "For Lou, a dream come true." November 28, 1985.
- "Kosar can choose draft—and team." April 24, 1985.
- "Lynn plans to name new coach this week." December 18, 1984.
- "Burns to resign after 16 years as Viking coach." November 7, 1984.

Sansevere, Bob, and Weiner, Jay. "Players express surprise and relief." *Minneapolis Star and Tribune* (newspapers.com). December 18, 1984.

Scheck, Tom. "Judge rules Twins can leave Metrodome after this season." Minnesota Public Radio (news.minnesota.publicradio.org). February 6, 2006.

Schmidt, Matthew. "The complete history of Kevin Garnett's beef with Timberwolves owner Glen Taylor." ClutchPoints (clutchpoints.com). April 10, 2020.

Schoenfield, David. "Still 30 teams: Contraction timeline." ESPN (espn.com). February 5, 2002.

Scoggins, Chip. *Star Tribune* (newspapers.com).
- "Pohlad has handcuffed future GM." July 19, 2016.
- "Despite 'total system failure,' Twins owner backs Ryan, Molitor." May 6, 2016.
- "U fires Mason, seeks new football 'vision.'" January 1, 2007.
- "A smack-down finish." October 16, 2005.
- "LSU wins bayou bounty." January 5, 2004.
- "Little Brown Ugh." October 11, 2003.
- "Valley Victory." September 28, 2003.

Schlossman, Brad Elliott. "NCAA Hockey: Holy Cross' upset that changed college hockey, 10 years later." NCAA (ncaa.com). March 24, 2016.

Seifert, Kevin. *Star Tribune* (newspapers.com).
- "Vikings decide not to wait and give walking papers to Smith." April 27, 2006.
- "Wilf gives Tice a quick boot." January 2, 2006.
- "Wilf vows Vikings will be first class on and off field." October 15, 2005.

- "Tice admits scalping." March 11, 2005.
- "Changes made in kicking game." October 24, 2002.
- "Gilliam falls, Brzezinksi rises in rank." April 26, 2002.
- "A big Vikings loss." February 8, 2001.
- "Cunningham now an ex-Viking." June 3, 2000.

Seifert, Kevin, and Barreiro, Dan. "Moss fine revealed." *Star Tribune* (newspapers.com). December 13, 2001.

Seifert, Kevin, and Youngblood, Kent. "Randle is released by Vikings." *Star Tribune* (newspapers.com). March 2, 2001.

Shelman, Jeff. "Gophers find Red Raiders unstoppable in the second half." *Star Tribune* (newspapers.com). December 30, 2006.

Sharp, Andrew. "Washington Senators I team ownership history." Society for American Baseball Research (sabr.org). Accessed May 21, 2020.

Showers, Bob. *Minnesota North Stars: History and Memories with Lou Nanne.* Beaver's Pond Press. October 1, 2007.

Siddiqui, Ali. "10 Years Later: Looking back at the Kevin Garnett trade." Dunking with Wolves (dunkingwithwolves.com). August 2, 2017.

Siems. "Written in Ice: A History of Pro Soccer in Minnesota – The Kicks." SB Nation: *Epluribus Loonum* (epluribusloonum.com). December 3, 2016.

Sinker, Howard. *Star Tribune* (newspapers.com).
- "Recalling Calvin Griffith's bigoted outburst in southern Minnesota." April 30, 2014.
- "So what happens now? Well, stay tuned." June 16, 1994.
- "No answers soon in 'U' investigation." April 28, 1988.
- "Griffith: Talk misunderstood." October 1, 1978.

Sinker, Howard, and Foley, Ellen. "The Met may fall, but memories will linger." *Star Tribune* (newspapers.com). January 29, 1985.

Sipple, George. "PSU could be a game changer." *Detroit Free Press* (newspapers.com). September 18, 2010.

Slovut, Gordon. "Glaucoma is an elusive threat to vision." *Star Tribune* (newspapers.com). April 25, 1996.

Smetanka, Mary Jane. "Gopher cheers to rise to roof, not skies." *Minneapolis Tribune* (newspapers.com). April 17, 1982.

Smith, Red. "As Super Bowl failure, Vikings are howling success." *Minneapolis Tribune* (newspapers.com). January 10, 1977.

Soucheray, Joe. *Minneapolis Tribune* (newspapers.com).
- "Minnesota is a downer for California draft choice." April 28, 1982.
- "Destructive fans bid violent adieu to Metropolitan Stadium." December 21, 1981.

- "Suddenly, big plays gone from Stars' game." May 15, 1981.
- "Sometimes it hurts to look in the mirror." May 13, 1981.
- "Joe Soucheray" (column). September 9, 1979.
- "Bobick is stopped by Norton in first." May 12, 1977.
- "Crowd's emotions erupt after Kicks' 3–1 victory." August 26, 1976.
- "Blyleven edged by Angels 3–2." June 1, 1976.

Souhan, Jim. *Star Tribune* (newspapers.com).
- "Graceful departure benefits coach and program he's leaving." March 21, 2018.
- "Confident leaders set high expectations for 2016." April 4, 2016.
- "Infield shows something sure was lost in translation." April 2, 2011.
- "Flying high." October 7, 2009.
- "Twins are building a contender—for 2010." February 3, 2008.
- "Vikings lost a lot when Gilliam was nudged out." June 17, 2007.
- "Pohlad should give as well as he receives." June 3, 2007.
- "One baseball fan offers kudos to all those behind the new Twins ballpark." May 22, 2006.
- "Owner doesn't feel guilty." October 7, 2002.
- "Selig offers little hope for Twins." November 16, 2001.
- "Vikings say little about Underwood." August 12, 1999.
- "Twins final out looms." November 7, 2001.
- "Downsizing the Twins." December 24, 1998.
- "Kirby says goodbye." July 13, 1996.
- "Puckett surgery: 'The big one.'" July 12, 1996.
- "Puckett out at least until August." June 26, 1996.
- "Vision problems might keep Puckett from Twins' opener." March 29, 1996.
- "Rider confronts his coach." December 11, 1994.
- "Holtz in Vikings' future?" November 19, 1991.

Souhan, Jim, and Slovut, Gordon. "Kirby's future? Still unclear." *Star Tribune* (newspapers.com). April 3, 1996.

Souhan, Jim, and Youngblood, Kent. "Vikings, Underwood agree to part ways." *Star Tribune* (newspapers.com). August 12, 1999.

Spagnola, Mickey. "A Pass and a Prayer: History of the Hail Mary." Dallas Cowboys (dallascowboys.com). November 8, 2019.

Spiros, Dean. *Star Tribune* (newspapers.com).
- "Holy Cross? Holy cow!" March 25, 2006.
- "No fire on the ice as Gophers lose again." March 19, 2006.

Stapleton, Arnie. "UMinn Scandal Escalates." ABC News (abcnews.go.com). January 7, 2006.

St. Anthony, Neal. "Billionaire Pohlad lived to deal." *Star Tribune* (newspapers.com). January 6, 2009.

Star News Services. "Expos deny demise." *The Windsor Star* (newspapers.com).
October 23, 2001.

Star Tribune (newspapers.com).
- "History of pro soccer in Minnesota." January 11, 2014.
- "Stadium concerts: A Twin Cities history." July 15, 2011.
- "Twins roll; 2,742 watch." September 7, 1995.
- "Memorial Stadium bricks selling well." August 3, 1992.
- "North Stars hockey player Dino Ciccarelli formally charged with indecent exposure." December 1, 1987.
- "Holtz again denies reports about Notre Dame." November 23, 1985.

Stark, Jayson, and Ford, Bob. "Baseball: The season is over, the Series out."
The Philadelphia Inquirer (newspapers.com). September 15, 1994.

Stensaas, Brian. "Randy Moss: A career timeline." *Star Tribune* (startribune.com).
February 3, 2018.

Stone, Doug. "Judge delays decision in Thompson case." *Minneapolis Tribune*
(newspapers.com). January 29, 1976.

Stoneking, Dan. *Minneapolis Star and Tribune* (newspapers.com).
- "Naming Holtz expected to help recruiting." December 23, 1983.
- "Suspensions group has many functions." January 29, 1972.

Stooge. "May 14, 1977—Shelley Duvall / Joan Armatrading (S2 E21)." The 'One
SNL a Day' Project (onesnladay.com). August 29, 2018.

Sullwold, Robert. "Court: Thompson can play for now." *Minneapolis Tribune*
(newspapers.com). February 12, 1976.

Swanson, Merrill. *Minneapolis Tribune* (newspapers.com).
- "Gopher second choice Musselman 'loves it.'" April 6, 1971.
- "Hill: Hazeltine Lacks 80 Acres of Corn, Cows." June 20, 1970.

Thompson, Denman. "Clark Griffith Buys Washington Ball Club." *The Sunday Star*
(newspapers.com). December 14, 1919.

Thorman, Joel. "Randy Moss Reportedly Told Vikings Owner That Brad Childress
Should Be Fired." SB Nation (sbnation.com). November 5, 2010.

Thornley, Stew. "Metropolitan Stadium (MN)." Society for American Baseball
Research (sabr.org). Accessed June 6, 2020.

"Timeline: Randy Moss through the years." *Pioneer Press* (twincities.com).
November 1, 2010.

Times Wire Services. "Dutcher Resigns, Minnesota Forfeits Game After
3 Arrests." *Los Angeles Times* (latimes.com). January 26, 1986.

Townsend, Brad. "It's been 30 years since the Cowboys traded Herschel Walker
to the Vikings, fueling a dynasty." *The Dallas Morning News* (dallasnews.com).
October 12, 2019.

University of Minnesota Athletics (gophersports.com).
- "3M Arena at Mariucci." Accessed June 8, 2020.
- "All-Time Attendance Records." Accessed June 8, 2020.
- "Gopher Sports Archives." Accessed June 8, 2020.
- "Men's Hockey: Archives." Accessed June 7, 2020.
- "Memorial Stadium (1924–81)." Accessed June 8, 2020.

"Vikings Franchise Timeline." Minnesota Vikings (vikings.com). Accessed May 24, 2020.

Van Wie, Dan. "The 50 Worst Regular-Season NFL Collapses in the Past 19 Years." Bleacher Report (bleacherreport.com). December 14, 2011.

Walsh, James, and Furst, Randy. "'Guilty plea' by 'U' paid off." *Star Tribune* (newspapers.com). October 25, 2000.

Walters, Charley, and Wittenmyer, Gordon. "Pohlad: Folding is really possible." *Pioneer Press* (twincities.com). November 1, 2001.

"WCHA History." WCHA (wcha.com). Accessed June 8, 2020.

"Weather History Archive." The Old Farmer's Almanac (almanac.com). Accessed June 9, 2020.

Webster, Danny. "David Ortiz Comments on Time with Twins, Release from Team, More." Bleacher Report (bleacherreport.com). March 19, 2016.

Weiner, Jay. *Stadium Games: Fifty Years of Big League Greed and Bush League Boondoggles*. University of Minnesota Press. March 13, 2001.

Weiner, Jay. *Star Tribune* (newspapers.com).
- "N.C. voters reject taxes to help build Twins ballpark." May 6, 1998.
- "Pohlad says he's not bluffing in negotiations to sell Twins." September 19, 1997.
- "Pohlad begins 'serious talks' with Carolina businessman." September 18, 1997.
- "Pohlad denies report of Charlotte offer." September 8, 1997.
- "Twins allowed to shop around." June 13, 1997.
- "'Quick fix' urged for Metrodome." September 12, 1995.
- "League questions Louisiana financing." June 16, 1994.
- "'U' men's basketball to be investigated." May 31, 1986.
- "Despite high wind, leaks, swaying lights, some panic, the Metrodome stayed up." April 28, 1986.
- "A year of upheaval, a season of controversy." December 18, 1984.
- "Holtz gives old hard sell for the dome." December 15, 1984.

Weiner, Jay, and Hartman, Sid. "League owners must OK any sale." *Star Tribune* (newspapers.com). May 24, 1994.

Wells, Mike. "Sprewell Wants Trade." *Pioneer Press* (twincities.com). November 1, 2004.

Wells, Nathan. "College hockey: Everything you need to know about the Frozen Four selection process." NCAA (ncaa.com). December 11, 2019.

Whereatt, Robert, and Weiner, Jay. "Pact aims to turn up heat on legislators." *Star Tribune* (newspapers.com). October 4, 1997.

"Who's Cheap?" *The Journal-News* (newspapers.com). August 17, 1983.

Windhorst, Brian. "Flip Saunders in, David Kahn out." ESPN (espn.com). May 2, 2013.

Wojnarowski, Adrian. "Kevin Love unsure about Timberwolves' future." Yahoo! Sports (sports.yahoo.com). December 11, 2012.

Wooden, John, and Yaeger, Don. *A Game Plan for Life*. Bloomsbury. March 8, 2011.

Wulf, Steve. "The run that birthed Dallas' dynasty." ESPN (espn.com). October 8, 2014.

"Yankees, Twins still dickering." *St. Petersburg Times* (newspapers.com). January 30, 1979.

Yotter, Tim. "Griffith doesn't doubt signal-stealing theory." 247 Sports (247sports.com). July 1, 2009.

Young, Lindsey. "Vikings, Seahawks Battle Through 3rd-Coldest Game in NFL History." Minnesota Vikings (vikings.com). January 10, 2016.

Youngblood, Kent. *Star Tribune* (newspapers.com).
- "Luck goes bust." May 19, 2015.
- "When Kicks were king." June 6, 2011.
- "Timberwolves owner: 'It hurts.'" August 1, 2007.
- "It's official: NFL rules Smith out for 2005." June 8, 2005.
- "Vikings rookie apologizes for departure from camp." August 4, 1999.

Zack, Margaret. "Boat party case against Culpepper dismissed." *Star Tribune* (newspapers.com). April 5, 2006.

Zavoral, Nolan. *Star Tribune* (newspapers.com).
- "Citing big losses, Strikers strike out." June 23, 1988.
- "New coach says he'll be own man—not Lou Holtz Jr." December 6, 1985.

Zgoda, Jerry. *Star Tribune* (newspapers.com).
- "Wiggins wears $148 million smile." October 12, 2017.
- "Going, going, gone." August 24, 2014.
- "So what's the point?" June 26, 2009.
- "Griffith makes an offer." September 15, 1998.
- "A Taylor-made solution." August 6, 1994.
- "Hockey, and a few fans, return." September 22, 1993.
- "The Wolves' choice is easy: Rider." July 1, 1993.
- "Wolves trade unhappy Mahorn to 76ers." October 28, 1989.

- "Wolves howl: Mahorn reaches agreement in Italy." October 20, 1989.
- "Mahorn, Corbin are top picks." June 16, 1989.
- "An era ends: Stars trade Ciccarelli, Rouse to Caps." March 8, 1989.
- "Ciccarelli, Stars reach agreement on contract." October 4, 1988.
- "Ciccarelli threatens to sit out—forever." September 7, 1988.
- "North Stars, Brooks part company." June 23, 1988.
- "Ciccarelli suspended 10 games." January 9, 1988.
- "Tie brings stars no relief." January 7, 1988.

Zinski, Dan. "Minnesota Vikings: Dennis Green left a mixed legacy." Fansided: The Viking Age (thevikingage.com). August 1, 2016.

Zulgad, Judd. *Star Tribune* (newspapers.com).
- "Prize or Surprise?" April 29, 2011.
- "Coach on the hot seat?" November 2, 2010.
- "Packers try to heal while Broncos rest." December 29, 2003.

Zulgad, Judd, and Furst, Randy. "Talk of eliminating Twins started as early as April '01." *Star Tribune* (newspapers.com). April 26, 2002.

A SPECIAL THANKS TO
VINTAGEMNHOCKEY.COM
FOR THE FIGHTING SAINTS PHOTO.

PHOTO CREDITS

ABOUT THE AUTHOR

Dan Whenesota is a lifelong Minnesotan and a lifelong sports fan. Some of his earliest sports memories are of collecting baseball cards and memorabilia with his father. His favorite team is the Vikings, but growing up, he watched and attended all sorts of sporting events: Twins, North Stars, Strikers, Timberwolves, Saints—and now the Wild, Lynx, and Loons, as well. He attended North Dakota State University and the University of Minnesota (and Macalester, Hamline, and Inver Hills). Dan is a teacher, coach, husband, father, computer nerd, and filmmaker, as well as a movie and TV junkie.

ABOUT DAN'S FILMS:

WHEN-ESOTA? is a documentary about the heartbreaks of being a Minnesota sports fan and why bad things keep happening to our beloved teams.

The North Star State is a documentary about the history of the Minnesota North Stars.

Both films are in development. Links to current drafts are available online via Dan's website.

WHENESOTA.COM · FACEBOOK.COM/WHENESOTA
TWITTER: @WHENESOTA · INSTAGRAM: @WHENESOTA

CPSIA information can be obtained
at www.ICGtesting.com
Printed in the USA
JSHW011518051120
9355JS00006B/6